FACING LONELINESS

Overseas Missionary
Fellowship
1058 Avenue Road
Toronto, Ontario M5N 2C6

Other books by Oswald J. Sanders
Prayer Power Unlimited
What of those who have never heard?

FACING LONELINESS

J. Oswald Sanders

HIGHLAND BOOKS

Copyright © Highland Books 1988

First published 1988

ISBN 0 946616 48 5

Printed in Great Britain for
HIGHLAND BOOKS
Broadway House, The Broadway
Crowborough, East Sussex TN6 1BY
by Richard Clay Ltd, Bungay
Typeset by CST, Eastbourne, East Sussex.

7.⁰⁰

CONTENTS

PREFACE

Loneliness is not a pleasant subject to write about. Nor is it a pleasant emotion to experience.

When I was asked to write on this subject, although the experience of twice losing a loved wife and 17 years spent as a widower had afforded personal experience of its poignancy, I shrank from the task. Others have done it, and doubtless done it better. But mounting experience with so many lonely souls in different lands and in different walks of life has impressed me deeply with the enormity and universality of the problem. And too few seem to have discovered a satisfying solution. So, reluctantly, I have taken up my pen, in the hope that something I write may help to ameliorate the pangs of loneliness for some readers.

I know there is no simplistic or single answer to the problem, no glib solution; for while the root cause is the same, the contributory factors are many. It is a complex phenomenon, and different types of loneliness require different approaches. Relief will be found only when we go beyond symptoms and deal with the toxic centre from which the

7

malady springs. The lack of intimacy, which is one of the most painful elements, must be redressed and remedied.

In the ultimate, loneliness stems from man's alienation from God, so no remedy which does not take this factor into account will afford more than superficial and temporary relief. But while the condition is rooted in the spiritual, the relevant psychological and social elements must not be overlooked.

The first part of the book is devoted mainly to an endeavour to isolate the causes of the malady, and the second to suggesting avenues of help for the individual needs of people. However, I have not confined the helpful suggestions to the second part.

The resources available to the lonely person, both from God and from fellow men and women, are more abundant than they realise and would discover if they made the attempt. Did they but realise it, their loneliness could be the starting-point of a new journey toward moral and spiritual maturity. If they would abandon the search for someone to care for them, and set themselves to care for someone else, they would be amazed to discover that their loneliness was quite bearable, even if it was not entirely banished.

PART I

ISOLATING THE CAUSES

1

DIAGNOSING THE MALADY

Diagnosis precedes prescription. It is only when the physician has made a correct diagnosis that he will be in a position to prescribe the appropriate remedy. It is no different with maladies of the spirit. Accordingly, the first section of this book aims at uncovering some of the causes of the universal malady of loneliness.

Loneliness is more readily experienced than defined. The Oxford Dictionary definition is: 'The state of having no companionship; being solitary; being dejected at the consciousness of being alone; being forlorn.' Taken together, these concepts combine to describe a bleak yet painfully common experience. It is not without reason that 'loneliness' has been termed the most desolate word in the English language. Its very sound seems to echo its own desolation.

One of its distressing features is that its victims are usually unable to diagnose the nature and source of their malady, and as a consequence are unable to discover an appropriate remedy. However, this should not discourage us from endeavouring to trace its tortuous course and hopefully discover ways in which its baneful effects can be ameliorated, or even totally eliminated.

Loneliness assumes many forms, each equally undesirable—an unsatisfied inner ache, an inner vacuum, a craving for satisfaction. The human heart has an insatiable longing to be loved.

Research has revealed that the experiences most conducive to the acute form are: the death of a life partner or other family member; a separation or divorce; a broken engagement; leaving one's homeland for a new country. All of these incur deep emotional trauma.

In other cases the loneliness unconsciously reflects a person's inability to initiate or maintain a stable and satisfying relationship, especially with members of the opposite sex. But whatever the cause, the experience is painful in the extreme.

At one of his crusades the Latin American evangelist, Luis Palau, asked the people in his audience to indicate the subject on which they would most like him to speak. A number of themes were suggested, but the majority requested him to speak on the subject of loneliness.

They were giving voice to the plight of many who suffer from one of the most pervasive and emotional disorders of our times. Its growing prevalence in the last half-century warrants careful investigation of both cause and possible cure. Of course loneliness has always plagued mankind, but the special conditions that prevail in our times have increased its incidence enormously.

One of the frequent side-effects is a sense of emptiness and futility which nothing seems to dispel.

Contemporary social and environmental factors are often the villain of the piece. For older people the breaking up of the family home, with the consequent loss of familiar friends and scenes, can prove a traumatic experience. They feel rootless and find it desperately difficult to strike up a new relationship in strange surroundings.

Irene Burnside contends that 'loneliness is the state of mind in which the fact that there were people in one's life in the past is more or less forgotten, and the hope that there may be inter-personal relations in the future is out of the realm of expectation.'[1]

It is no sin to be lonely, so there is no need to add a sense of guilt to the problem. Our sinless Lord was lonely. But if the facts of the case are not faced realistically and purposefully, harmful attitudes may develop which will hinder present enjoyment of life and fruitful service for God and man in the future.

THE SEED-PLOT OF LONELINESS

It is rather surprising to discover that despite its universality in past ages as well as in our own, loneliness is nowhere treated at length in the Bible. Illustrations of its ravages, however, abound. The Scriptures alone provide us with a credible and authentic diagnosis of man's fundamental problems, so it must be to the Bible we look for both diagnosis and cure.

The biblical record asserts that in his original state, Adam, the first man, was perfect in form and intelligence.

'God created man in his own image,
in the image of God he created him;
male and female he created them . . .
God saw all that he had made and it
was very good' (Gen 1.27, 31).

But though he came perfect from the hand of
God, Adam was still finite and incomplete. This is
implicit in the first recorded statement from the
mouth of God.

'The Lord said, *it is not good for the
man to be alone.* I will make a helper
suitable for him . . . The Lord God
caused the man to fall into a deep
sleep, and while he was sleeping, he
took one of the man's ribs and closed
up the place with flesh. Then the
Lord God made a woman from the
rib he had taken out of the man, and
he brought her to him' (Gen 2.18, 21,
22: *italics mine*).

In their original innocence, Adam and Eve lived
without shame or fear. They enjoyed uninhibited
companionship with each other and with the Lord
God. They were neither alone nor lonely.

Into this idyllic scene the serpent subtly insinuated
himself and successfully seduced them into sin.
This, in turn, resulted in the forfeiture of their per-
fection and innocence, for it was an act of rebellion
against their Creator and Benefactor. Henceforth
they were fallen beings, and involved the whole
human race in their fall. But although the image of

God in them was sadly defaced, it was not totally obliterated. *In that pregnant moment loneliness was born.*

The immediate result of their sin and folly was banishment from the Garden of Eden. Henceforth they were enmeshed in the tentacles of fear and gripped by the icy fingers of loneliness. Tragic exchange! Desolating loneliness for intimacy with God!

MAN'S TWOFOLD NEED
Man was created with a twofold need—fellowship with God and companionship with other human beings. For these, if he is to realise the full purpose of his creation, there can be no substitute. The social instinct is innate in every human being and when this need remains unsatisfied, the seeds of loneliness grow and flourish.

We are vulnerable to the onslaught of loneliness on a number of levels, of which the *emotional* is the most distressing because it involves the loss of close relationship with other people. It can be relieved only by establishing some alternative, congenial association. To those who are by nature shy or reserved, this presents an almost insuperable obstacle.

Social loneliness is related to the contacts we have—or do not have—with the community in which we live. There is a chronic sense of being 'left out', and this in turn generates a feeling of low self-worth. The victim labours under the conviction—by no means always justified—that he or she is of little significance to anyone, and therefore no one desires his friendship. This attitude often issues in a largely self-imposed isolation.

What people in this state of mind most need is a group of caring and supportive friends; but how and where can they find them? In many churches this need is met in home groups, whose members exercise a mutual interest in the others' welfare. But the initial step—the joining of such a group—is in the decision of the sufferer.

Poignant though social loneliness undoubtedly is, *spiritual loneliness* is even more fundamental to the condition, for it carries with it the feeling of isolation, not only from fellow men and women, but from the God who alone can fill the vacuum in the human heart.

Blaisé Pascal, the noted French scientist, held that in every human heart there exists a God-shaped vacuum. Centuries before him, Augustine, Bishop of Hippo, put his finger on the root cause of loneliness in the oft-repeated words: 'God created man for Himself and our hearts are restless until they find rest in Him.'

For this reason, the greatest need of the lonely person is to ensure that he or she is in a right relationship with God, the Great Physician. He has a panacea for every lack and malady of the human heart, whether it be spiritual or social.

CONTRIBUTORY CAUSES

In our indulgent and affluent western society, where most can gratify their every desire, it seems inexplicable that so many are victims of the scourge of loneliness and that it is as prevalent among the rich as among the poor. Many factors have combined to produce this effect.

Sweeping changes in the social structures of society

have contributed their quota. *Unprecedented mobility* on and and in the air has abetted this trend. The illusion that the grass is greener on the other side of the fence, is reflected in the fact that every year 20 per cent of a community living in an urban situation change their location. This inevitably precipitates the break-up of family groups and hinders the development of a community spirit and the forming of enduring friendships.

Modern technology and the magic of the microchip have added immeasurably to the complexity and yet uniformity of modern life. Everything tends to grow more impersonal. The old corner store, with its personal attention and service, has disappeared before the relentless competition of the supermarket. The mass-production line has reduced many skilful workers to the status of human robots. The competent tradesman who used to take a pride in his work has been made redundant, or forced into early retirement. In an increasingly automated world, people tend to become mere numbers and have fewer opportunities of forming close personal associations. One unwilling retiree expressed his feelings:

> *'Since I have retired from life's*
> *competition*
> *Each day is filled with complete*
> *repetition.*
> *I get up each morning and dust off my*
> *wits,*
> *Go, pick up the paper and read*
> *the obits.*
> *If my name isn't there, I know I'm*

not dead,
I get a good breakfast and go
back to bed.'

Paradoxically, the *rapid urbanisation* of the world
—a modern phenomenon which has spawned 300
cities of more than one million citizens—while forc-
ing people to live closer together physically, has
resulted in even greater social isolation. In China,
according to the census taken in 1982, only about 20
per cent of the people lived in city centres. By 1986
the proportion had shot up to 37 per cent.

The stark high-rise apartment blocks of the
mega-cities are characterised more by fear and sus-
picion than by friendship and neighbourliness.
There are, of course, glorious exceptions to this
generalisation, but it is, sadly, very near the truth.
Is it not a strange anomaly that large numbers of
people can live cheek by jowl, and yet at the same
time be gripped by intense loneliness? Yet such is
the case.

THE TELEVISION INVASION

Television has proved a very mixed blessing. Like
many other inventions that have great potential for
good, television has been exploited—one could say
prostituted—by greedy and unprincipled people for
selfish and often evil purposes. One of its baneful
effects is that habitual viewers seldom communicate
with one another in a meaningful way. Superficial
viewing habits are formed which inhibit intelligent
conversation and deep thought.

A great many of the programmes presented are
not merely inane, but positively harmful. Violence

and pornography slip through the censor's net and intrude uninvited into the homes of the people. As a direct consequence we are reaping the harvest in a sharply rising rate of crime.

Altogether apart from these crudely adverse features, viewers are encouraged to live in a world of fantasy and unreality. Instead of enjoying genial and congenial action and interaction with family and friends, many live their lives vicariously in the lives of the television actors and actresses, be they good or bad. When parents who are concerned about the mental and moral standards presented to their children attempt to monitor the programmes, the result is very often family discord.

These, and many of the factors involved in the television invasion, combine to provide a fertile culture-bed for loneliness.

LONELINESS IS UNIVERSAL

'It is strange to be known so universally, and yet to be so lonely.' These poignant words were spoken by the great scientist Albert Einstein, and demonstrate that loneliness invades the lives of the great and intellectual as well as those of people in lower stations of life. It is no respecter of persons. But perhaps it was Einstein's very brilliance that isolated him from lesser mortals and gave birth to his loneliness.

Perhaps more than at any time in history, this scourge has become endemic in the world and not less in the sophisticated than in primitive societies. It is not an unusual phenomenon that is confined to a few constitutionally solitary souls. Rather is it a rapidly increasing element of human existence, an inescapable fact of life, part of the human predicament. It seems to keep pace with the rapidity of social and industrial change in today's world. It has been accurately described as a 'debilitating deficiency disease that knows no limitations of age, class, or sex.'

An American newspaper, concerned to discover the type of problem that was of most concern to its readers, conducted a wide survey. In the responses received, three problems predominated. They were, in order of priority—fear, worry, loneliness. It is worthy of note that in the last of the three, there are elements of the first two as well. But it is loneliness that casts the longest shadow on our contemporary world.

In a poll conducted among patients in a psychiatric hospital, almost 80 per cent claimed that it had been loneliness that had driven them to seek help from the psychiatrist. It is small wonder that David Jeremiah termed it, 'the disease of the decade, perhaps of every decade in our mid and late 20th century.'[2]

A large number of modern pop songs and lyrics are shot through with the melancholy themes of frustration, emptiness, loneliness. Much of the accompanying music is set in the minor key and is a reflection of the negative aspects of life. Country and western music majors in broken relationships, desertion and infidelity. All of which tells its own story.

'Once a philosophical problem contemplated by poets and prophets, loneliness is now a universal condition for millions of Americans. Not only for the elderly and divorced, but also for the men and women *filled with the ache of loneliness within their marriages*. It is fast becoming an American tradition.'[3]

So runs the blurb on the cover of the book by Tim Timmons, *Loneliness is not a Disease*.

THE RACIAL MIX

The impact of the electronic age, the widening reach of the media and communications, and burgeoning population in many nations, have thrown men and women together to a degree never before experienced. The racial mix in many mega-cities is well-nigh incredible. The author was speaking recently with the headmaster of a high school in Los Angeles. He said that among his student body no fewer than 52 ethnic groups were represented! Pity the teachers!

Instead of eliminating loneliness, as one would expect, this inescapable contact of the races has served only to exacerbate it. There seems to be little desire in most ethnic groups to overleap racial and cultural barriers. Too often it is a case of physical proximity without emotional intimacy.

Foreign students in western lands are exceptionally vulnerable to the ravages of this malady. An African student, who attended a British university, opened his heart to a sympathetic listener and poured out his lonely experience as he struggled to adapt to an alien culture:

'At home, I walk along, my eyes raised, meeting the eyes of the people coming along the road towards me—neighbours, family, friends. We call out, we greet one another. Here in Britain I walk along your streets. People's eyes do not meet mine. They look away, avoiding my glance. No one greets me, no one calls out. Everyone seems to be rushing, silent.'[4]

How deep and poignant was this man's loneliness! And he is representative of thousands in like case.

A student in one university carved a pathetic question on his desk: 'Why am I so lonely when there are two thousand here?' He was learning the painful lesson that there can be close physical contact without meaningful relationship.

'Yes, in the sea of life enisled,
With echoing straits between us thrown,
Dotting the shoreless watery world,
We mortals live alone.'

Matthew Arnold

2

SOLITUDE IS NOT LONELINESS

'It is nothing new to be lonely. It comes to all of us sooner or later . . . If we try to retreat from it, we end in a darker hell. But if we face it, if we remember that there are a million others like us, if we reach out and try to comfort them and not ourselves, we find in the end that we are lonely no longer.'[1]

Morris West

While there are points of similarity between solitude and loneliness, it is quite wrong to equate them without qualification. It is true that the two at times do coalesce, but neither the words nor the experience are synonymous.

The word 'alone' occurs frequently in the Bible, but only in very few cases can it be equated with loneliness. Our Lord differentiated the two concepts when He said, 'You will leave me all alone. Yet I am not alone for my Father is with me' (Jn 16.32). The different significance of the two words has been expressed in this way: *Loneliness* is the result of the absence of personal intimacy or meaningful activity. *Solitude* is not being in the company of others.

Loneliness is always and essentially a negative experience, while solitude often is positive and renewing. It can generate a sense of solitariness that is both creative and motivating, while loneliness brings a feeling of desolation and depression that can be destructive. It tends to stifle hope and quench aspiration. The one is involuntary, coming unbidden. The other is voluntary and decisively chosen.

John Milton drew attention to the fact that loneliness was the first thing that God saw was not good: 'It is not good for the man to be alone.' But there are times when the hard-pressed heart craves solitude more than anything else.

> *'I wish*
> *That I could enter in*
> *And close the door*
> *Of my small house*
> *To dwell alone*
> *As little shellfish do.'*

Mumei

Following on His assertion that loneliness was not good for Adam (Gen 2.18), God created 'a helper suitable for him.' So thus early in human history, God indicated that man was made for companionship, not isolation. He was created a social being, capable of sustaining loving and congenial relationships with both God and his fellow men and women. The full purpose of his creation can never be realised in isolation, only in association with other men and women. Because we are gregarious by nature, the absence of a friend or companion creates an emotional vacuum which can work havoc on both body and spirit. When the late Duke of Windsor abdicated the throne of Britain in order to marry the woman he loved, but who was not acceptable to the Royal Family, he went into a self-imposed exile. As a result of his own bitter experience he declared that loneliness was not simply a matter of being alone, but rather the feeling that no one really cares what happens to you. It is not necessarily caused by a set of circumstances—it is a state of mind.

Harry Sisler betrayed real insight into the inwardness of the problem when he wrote:

> *'The human spirit seems doomed to*
> *live alone.*
> *That which we share is but the threshold*
> *Of the habitation of our being. Still*
> *unshown*
> *Are the deeply hidden qualities which*
> *enfold.*
> *That which is truly us we don't dis-*
> *close.'*

Being alone involves only physical separation, but *being lonely* includes both spiritual and psychological isolation. It produces a solitude of heart, the feeling of being cut off from others whom we would like to have as friends.

As has been said, a certain degree of solitude—being alone with one's thoughts—is a normal state.

It is essential to the culture of the inner life. We all experience times when it becomes essential to escape from 'the madding crowd's ignoble strife,' and engage in constructive introspection (in contrast to the morbid type). Without such periodic physical withdrawal, the spiritual life will lack depth and freshness. In such a period of solitude we will find a welcome alternative to the rat-race of modern life.

'Most of us are so engrossed in making a living,' said one writer, 'that we do not stop to think whether we are making a life.' We need to be alone in order to discover and confront our real selves. A time of self-imposed solitude has often led to invaluable self-analysis and a fresh outlook on life.

CONSTRUCTIVE SOLITUDE

Periods of loneliness, if used in a ruthlessly honest manner, can equip us to help others who find themselves facing the same problem. It should be observed that our Lord's frequent desire for solitude was not for the mere sake of being alone; it was primarily to enjoy communion with His Father. Then, strengthened and encouraged by that fellowship, He returned better equipped to meet the demands of the needy and lonely crowds that constantly thronged Him. 'The servant is not greater than his Lord.'

Far from being an unwelcome liability, solitude confers many fringe benefits. It is in the place of quietness that creativity flourishes, not in the hurly-burly of modern life. We are so constituted that while we crave intimacy with other human beings, there are times when solitude becomes imperative, *especially the silence of aloneness with God,* when other voices have died away. It is then we have the unique opportunity of listening unhurriedly to His 'voice of gentle stillness.' The enrichment that follows cannot be exaggerated, for communion with the Eternal God is the most potent medium of inner fulfilment.

The need for quietness and solitude was never greater than it is today. Dr A.W. Tozer writes that some of God's children want to relearn the ways of solitude and simplicity. 'They want to discover the blessedness of spiritual aloneness.' To such he offered this counsel: 'Retire from the world each day to some private spot . . . Stay in the secret place till the surrounding noises begin to fade out of your heart and a sense of God's presence envelops you. Deliberately tune out the unpleasant sounds and come out of your closet determined not to hear them. Listen for the inward Voice till you learn to recognise it . . . Learn to pray inwardly every moment. After a while you can do this even while you work.'[2]

> *'Thank you, God, for making restful silence,*
> *Loveliest of all the sounds I hear.*
> *My ears are aching and my body tenses,*
> *Too many sounds, too loud, too near.'*

REGAINING HEAVEN'S PERSPECTIVE

Solitude affords the needed opportunity of *regaining heaven's perspective* on the mysteries of life. This was the experience of Asaph the psalmist, who opens his heart and shares his perplexity in Psalm 73.

As he surveyed the world around him and observed the prosperity of the wicked people among whom he moved, he almost lost his faith. He was mystified that God should allow them to prosper and profit by their evil deeds, while often the good people appeared to have more than their share of adversity and suffering. Was God really being fair in acting in that way? In the light of His seeming injustice, Asaph had begun to wonder what was the point and profit of being righteous.

J. Russell Lowell might have had Asaph's plaint in mind when he wrote his well-known lines:

> 'Careless seems the great Avenger,
> History's pages but record
> One death-grapple in the darkness
> 'Twixt old systems and the Word.
> Truth for ever on the scaffold,
> Wrong for ever on the throne.'

Hear Asaph as he pours out his complaint:

> 'As for me, my feet had almost slipped, I had nearly lost my foothold, for I envied the arrogant when I saw the prosperity of the wicked. They have no struggles; their bodies are healthy and strong. They are free from the burdens common to man; they are not plagued by human ills . . . This is what the wicked are like— always carefree, they increase in wealth . . . Surely in vain have I kept my heart pure . . . When I tried to

understand all this it was oppressive to me *till I entered the sanctuary of God; then I understood . . .'* (Ps 73. 2–5, 16, 17: *italics mine*).

It was not until he repaired to the silence of the sanctuary of God that heaven's perspective once again gained the ascendancy and he found a fresh foothold for his faith. It was there that the truth enshrined in Lowell's following lines gripped his soul:

> *'Yet that scaffold sways the future,*
> *And behind the dim unknown*
> *Standeth God within the shadows,*
> *Keeping watch above His own.'*

Habakkuk the prophet was equally mystified and for the same reason as Asaph, as he looked at the world around him from his lonely watch-tower:

> 'How long, O Lord, must I call for help, but you do not listen? Or cry out to you 'Violence!' but you do not save? Why do you make me look at injustice? Why do you tolerate wrong?' (Hab 1.2, 3).

'Like many today,' writes W.S. Hooton, 'he seems to have found it difficult to reconcile with the divine government the triumphs of the wicked and treacherous over those who, whatever their sins, were not so laden with guilt. The sins of God's people had called for correction (1.12), and the

29

prophet knew where their refuge was to be found.'[3]

Where did he find the answer to his perplexity? In his watch-tower, when he listened for the voice of God.

In the rush of our pressured lives it is easy to allow the world to dictate our agenda, to squeeze us into its mould, while we ourselves are unconscious of the subtle erosion of our own standards and values. Jesus did not allow even the clamant need and suffering of the masses around to rob Him of those precious times of quiet. They were sacred oases in the desert of human sin.

He identified Himself so thoroughly with our humanity that *He experienced acute loneliness*—one of the sinless infirmities which He voluntarily assumed at the Incarnation. It was no surprise to Him when His disciples all forsook Him and fled. Had He not already forewarned them of that danger? And they deserted Him in His hour of greatest need. But in that darkest hour of His loneliness, He confessed His unshaken confidence in His Father's abiding presence:

> 'You will leave me all alone. *Yet I am
> not* alone, for my Father is with me'
> (Jn 16.32: *italics mine*).

This joyous fact more than compensated for the absence of human companionship. *He knew the ultimate panacea for loneliness, and so may we.*

Let the desolate soul take comfort from the fact that God is just as really present with His lonely children today as He was with His Son. But it is only as we believe and appropriate that fact, that we will enjoy the blessing and benefit of His conscious presence.

Out of his rich experience of walking with God, Thomas à Kempis gave this advice concerning the value of solitude:

> 'Watch for good times to retreat into yourself. Frequently meditate on how good God is to you. Skip the tricky questions. Read things which move your heart. If you will stop gossiping and chattering, you will find plenty of time for helpful meditation.
> 'You will find in your closet prayer what you frequently lose when you are out in the world. The more you visit it, the more you will want to return. But the more you avoid it, the harder it will be to come back.'[4]

TRANSFORMING SOLITUDE

> 'And Jacob was left alone' (Gen 32. 25).

These five words have a plaintive ring about them. But in the encounter that ensued, Jacob discovered to his great surprise that he was alone with the very God who, for two decades, had been pursuing him with undiscouraged ardour, with the sole purpose of blessing him. And now he has painted himself into a corner.

In order to soften up the brother whom he had so shamefully defrauded, Jacob had sent on ahead his wife, children and flocks, together with lavish presents for Esau. And now he was all alone!

How he dreaded the hour of confrontation with his brother! Little did he dream that this unplanned hour of solitude would be fraught with unimagined blessing. He had to learn that God never gives up in His desire to bless his erring children.

> '*Come, O Thou Traveller unknown,*
> *Whom still I hold but cannot see,*
> *My company before is gone,*
> *And* I am left alone with Thee!
> *With Thee all night I mean to stay,*
> *And wrestle till the break of day.*'
>
> Charles Wesley

But the words 'left alone' can hold different connotations to different people. For some they spell longed-for rest and quietness, for others only aching loneliness. To be *left alone without God* is hell. But to be *left alone with God* is a foretaste of heaven.

It was only when Jacob the deceiver was shut up alone with God that he was transformed into Israel the prince, who now had *power with God and man*. What marvellous grace on the part of God! One could conceive of our generous God granting him the privilege of having influence with his fellowmen. This would be an incredible expression of divine forgiveness and restoration. But to 'have power *with God*?' Only a God as great and as gracious as our God could have conceived such an act of love and grace.

SOLITUDE IS NOT LONELINESS

'Lame as I am, I take the prey,
*   Hell, earth and sin with ease*
*   o'ercome,*
I leap for joy, pursue my way,
*   And as a bounding hart fly home.*
Through all eternity to prove,
Thy nature and Thy name is love.'

Charles Wesley

3

NO AGE-GROUP IMMUNE

In his inimitable way, Shakespeare has depicted in
The Seven Ages of Man the distinctive character
traits of the individual at each stage of life. A similar
progression may be seen in man's spiritual pilgrimage. Each stage of life's ongoing development has
its own peculiar characteristics. Unfortunately it is
also true that from childhood to old age, loneliness
is present and tends to assume a different form in
each era of life. No age-bracket is immune from its
ravages.

Young children can experience loneliness very
early in life. In his *Fear of Love,* Ira J. Tanner
says, 'Loneliness has its beginning in childhood,
sometimes between the ages of one and three. It is
a root condition of life, and it is during these post-
embryonic years that we first begin to experience
doubt as to our self-worth.'

Childish emotions are doubtless more fleeting
than those of adults, but to the child they are painfully real at the time. The shy child, for example,
suffers agonies when separated from its mother on
the first day at school. In the same way the back-

ward or unpopular child, or one with some physical deformity, will feel rejected, left out, unwanted.

It is not uncommon for young children from *broken homes* to feel that in some way they are to blame for the family tragedy. Especially is this so when the child has been at the centre of the parental dispute. Other children are lonely because their parents spend so little time with them, or are insensitive to their need of affection. The greatly reduced time two working parents are able to spend with their children creates an emotional vacuum in the child's heart. Obsession with TV on the part of either parent or child reduces still further the amount of quality family time enjoyed.

With some sensitive children, misunderstandings or fear of punishment may cause them to take refuge in withdrawal, or to live in a world of fantasy. One nine-year-old boy was playing with his friends recently when accidentally he started a fire that did some damage. As he had been warned by his mother not to play with matches, he was afraid to own up to his involvement.

When his mother asked him if he had been involved, he flatly denied it. However, from his subsequent withdrawn attitude his parents were convinced that he had played some part in the fire. But again he steadfastly denied it. But when his mother assured him that if he had started the fire and confessed it, he would not be punished, he broke down and acknowledged his part in the incident. It was a very relieved little boy who burst out of the ice-house of loneliness his denial had erected.

Surprisingly, researchers have discovered that *adolescents and young adults* tend to be more acutely lonely than do the elderly.[1] This springs, in part, from the desperate need they feel to be socially accepted, especially by their peers. They have reached the in-between stage when they feel identity with neither child nor adult. This results in their feeling unable to discover a niche into which they can fit comfortably. One survey revealed that loneliness is the biggest problem confronting teenagers today.

Naturally enough they want to be individuals in their own right. I remember my son telling me that in his early adolescence he did not want to be known merely as my son, he wanted to be himself—a perfectly natural stage of development.

It is at this point that many young people become estranged from their parents and throw off restraint. In their loneliness they hunger for understanding and acceptance. If this is not extended to them at home, they seek it elsewhere, sometimes in questionable places.

Excessive noise and frenzied activity seem to be an essential element in contemporary adolescent behaviour patterns. Adults do not always appreciate the result, and when objection is taken to the excess of decibels, the young person feels rejected and disapproved and retreats into his loneliness.

All these factors combine to produce an acute loneliness that sometimes finds expression in anti-social behaviour. It is not without significance that the suicide rate among adolescents has doubled in recent years.

One researcher reported that, 'Although some suicides are drug-induced, most youthful suicides or attempted suicides have a history of unhappiness, fears or loneliness behind them. Those who look to suicide as a solution, already feel alone in the world.'[2]

In their rebellion against parental restrictions some young people try to drown their loneliness in alcohol or drugs, or by flouting the standards and culture of their family in both dress and behaviour. In this way they hope to find acceptance with a more congenial group, even though they are 'way out.' It is among these young people that the greatest problems of law enforcement are encountered.

The only child faces yet another type of loneliness. In order to ward off its pangs, he often withdraws into a world of fantasy. If he does not happen to be creative or imaginative, and able to make his own amusement, he finds himself living, in the main, in an adult world. This in turn makes it more difficult for him to form easy relationships with his peers in the world of reality.

The adopted child who is aware of that fact faces yet another set of problems. He has to deal with that peculiar type of loneliness that is generated by a lack of identity. Who are his parents? Why did they abandon him? Why was he not wanted? Is he illegitimate? Kind though the adoptive parents may be, the often unanswered questions leave their mark on a sensitive and lonely heart.

Old people are expected to be lonely! But it is a great mistake to lump them all together and equate old age with loneliness. Research discloses that many old people fare much better in this respect than do their younger counterparts. For this there are valid reasons. Loneliness usually takes young people by surprise. Older people, on the other hand, are more conditioned to expect to be lonely in some degree.

As time passes they discover that most of their contemporaries are having somewhat parallel experiences, and so they are more likely to take their condition philosophically. In all honesty it must be confessed, however, that these are not in the majority. A greater number of the aged are desperately lonely. For them life seems to hold little meaning, especially if they are housebound. They feel neither needed nor wanted, and this is one of the most poignant aspects of old age. Everyone wants to feel needed.

Mother Teresa of Calcutta has spent her life working among the poor and lepers of that tragic city—probably the poorest people in the world. In accepting the Nobel Prize, which she was awarded for her amazing sacrificial service, she said that she had come more and more to realise that it is *being unwanted that is the worst disease any human being can ever experience*. Disease of the spirit is more serious than disease of the body.

For many elderly people—especially men—television is the most important factor in their lives, for it helps pass the weary, pointless hours less monotonously. But at best it is a one-way street. It demands no response. All it requires is passive observation, and the old saying proves too true: impression without expression brings depression.

Those confined in nursing homes are lonely because they are separated from friends and relatives, sometimes in an enviroment that is far from congenial. Because many of their companions are well advanced along the road to senility, stimulating conversation is at a premium.

Not long ago I was having lunch with a friend who had entered her second century. I was amused when she took me by the arm and led me away.

'Come and let us have some intelligent conversation,' she said. 'I hardly ever have sensible conversation with the others in the nursing home.' To those whose powers are still sharp and functioning, such an atmosphere must be depressing.

There are few for whom *the crisis of retirement,* whether voluntary or enforced, does not create some degree of emotional upheaval. The loss of congenial companionship and status that usually accompanies retirement, tends to generate a loss of self-worth as well. A decreasing contact with familiar society can leave the retiree without a stimulating goal or congenial occupation. The cheerful backchat enjoyed with business associates or workmates is sorely missed, and life descends into dull monotony.

For *the busy mother,* a new crisis is reached when the last child leaves the parental roof. This can be for her just as traumatic an experience as her husband's retirement from business life is to him. The once noisily happy home suddenly becomes a sombre vacuum. Life loses its significance and motivation is lacking. Unless she can find some meaningful substitute activity, loneliness will inevitably take over. Fortunately, it is often at this stage of life that the advent of grandchildren breaks the pattern.

For *the Christian,* retirement years should be viewed as a divinely given and valuable opportunity for new adventure and achievement. The best days do not all lie in the past. The years of lifted responsibility should be regarded only as a junction, not a terminus, an exciting new beginning, even a new career. It has proved to be so in many cases.

> *'While closing days leave something to*
> *do,*
> *Some deeper truth to learn, some gift*
> *to gain,*
> *Let me with cheerful mind my path*
> *pursue,*
> *And thankful, glean the fragments that*
> *remain.'*
>
> T.D. Bernard

But not everyone embraces such an outlook. Contrast that optimistic outlook on life's closing days with that which Lord Byron depicts in his *Childe Harold*:

> *'What is the worst of foes that wait on*
> *age?*
> *What stamps the wrinkle deeper on the*
> *brow?*
> *To view each loved one blotted from*
> *life's page,*
> *And be as I am now.'*

But elderly people or retirees need not feel that their days of significant contribution are in the past. There is no need for them to resign themselves to lonely purposelessness. Though they may be less active physically than of old, there is no reason why their closing years should not be even more influential in another way. Through the years they have acquired a store of wisdom and experience which they can share with the rising generation.

This was the outlook of the psalmist in Psalm 71.18:

> 'Since my youth, O God, you have taught me, and to this day I declare your marvellous deeds. Even when I am old and gray, do not forsake me, O God, till I declare your power to the next generation, your might to all who are to come.'

Longfellow recognised the possibility of continuing fruitfulness in old age when he wrote:

> *'For age is opportunity, no less*
> *Than youth itself, though in another*
> *dress;*
> *And as the evening twilight fades away,*
> *The sky is filled with stars*
> *   Invisible by day.'*

4

THE NUCLEAR FAMILY

The changes in current social structures have laid us open to the inroads of loneliness to a much greater degree than was the case in earlier years. Even as recently as last century, the great majority of homes were multi-generational. Both social functions and religious activity had their focus in the home. Children were born there, with friends and relatives around the expectant mother—a far cry from the sterile, impersonal maternity hospital. Deaths occurred there, and funerals were conducted from the family home, not from the commercial 'funeral home.'

While this was not without its problems, the result of the inevitably close interaction was to make the family a well-integrated unit, whose members laughed and cried, worked and played together—again a far cry from the experience of today's so-called 'nuclear family.'

Even in such a close-knit community it was possible for family members to be painfully lonely. But the chances were against it. Today the whole picture is reversed. Instead of being the centre of family life, the home has become, in the main, a point of departure—to school, to work, to sport, to social activities, to church. Even on those occasions when the family is together, television has reduced relaxed and happy communication to a minimum. It is the favourite serial or sports item that claims pride of place.

Today's *'nuclear family,'* consisting of father, mother and one or two children, has replaced the multi-generational family of the last century. This radical social change carries within itself the seeds of its own desolation; for as the current generation is proving, present sociological conditions are a fertile culture-bed for acute loneliness.

Imagine the loneliness of the single child now permitted to Chinese parents. In their efforts to contain the population explosion, the Chinese authorities have erased two words from their vocabulary—brother and sister. Most Chinese children of the recent generation have neither.

The ever-increasing *mobility and restlessness* of our society, consequent upon the advent of car and aeroplane, tends to increase the problem. It is estimated that in many communities more than one family in five changes its location every year. Add to this the fact that because of economic conditions a diminishing number of families now own their own home, and we have a situation in which it is difficult for families to put down deep roots. There is also an industrial fluidity that causes people to keep moving in the hope of gaining stability and financial security in more congenial circumstances.

In many countries, *immigration* and the influx of refugees and foreign seasonal workers add another dimension and increase the community of the lonely. The ethnic mix, with its consequent linguistic confusion, constitutes another isolating factor. Many of the student children of the first generation of immigrants, who have been torn from their own familiar culture, find the adjustment painful in the extreme.

In the bustling republic of Singapore, almost three-quarters of the population live in small apartments in towering high-rise buildings. This is the pattern of living that is emerging in the burgeoning cities of many developing nations.

This congested mode of communal living, however, militates against the likelihood of warm and enduring relationships being established with other families in the complex. Very few get to know their fellow-tenants in more than a casual manner. Families live in isolation, and the prevalent mood of restlessness makes it easy to pack up and move to another location, which usually proves equally lonely. Apartment-dwelling has been found to inhibit the formation of those close relationships so essential to the wholesome development of a growing family.

The rapid *acceleration of urbanisation* in most countries of the world necessarily involves the severing of agelong family ties, leaving behind the familiar culture and moving into a large, impersonal and unwelcoming city to face an unknown future. It takes no vivid imagination to envisage the trauma involved in such a situation.

The latest demographic reports reveal that there are now 300 cities of more than one million inhabitants, and the sobering fact is that the majority of these cities are in the economically distressed developing countries which are at least able to cope with the resulting problems. Of necessity this means for many who leave their rural situations, a loss of identity, of roots.

Because of economic necessity, in the majority of families in these cities both parents are at work, a condition which has become the norm, not the exception. This results in a minimum amount of time families can spend together in relaxed fun and fellowship. Youth centres and sports activities claim much of the free time of young people, and each member of the family spends far more time away from home, even in leisure hours.

A further word on the impact of television on the family is appropriate, for there is no doubt that it has played a significant part in producing loneliness. It has changed the face of society, and not all for the better. On the whole, it has had a deleterious effect on family togetherness. Ordinary conversation between family members is reduced to a minimum. Children cease to communicate freely with parents, sitting instead with eyes glued to the fascinating box. Attempts to limit viewing time or monitor programmes are either futile or cause unpleasantness.

The vast impact of television on the average child of our times may be learned from the fact that in the course of his lifetime, he or she will spend up to 15,000 viewing hours in the lonely world of TV!

Nielsons, the research company whose ratings determine the fate of America's film and video fare, provide these startling facts concerning the influence of the media on home and family. During the 1977–1978 season, the average American household watched TV for an estimated time of 6¼ hours a day. By 1980 the watching period increased to 7¼ hours. As 95 per cent of Japanese homes have colour television, a similar position in all probability exists there.

Vladimir Kosma Zworykin, the Russian-born inventor of television, said on his ninety-first birthday, 'I would never let my children even come close to this thing.'

Neil Postman, professor of communications at a New York university, was reported in *US News and World Report* as maintaining that TV, as a curriculum, moulds the intelligence and character of youth far more than formal schooling. How important, then, that they view the right programmes.

Malcolm Muggeridge, who was at one time Britain's foremost television interviewer, on page 18 of his book *The End of Christendom* caustically expressed his view of the effect of television on family and community:

> 'Consider our excessive and obsessive televiewing. The average modern man looks at television for four hours every day, which means that he spends ten years of his life looking into the television screen; something that precludes reading, conversation and other exercises in literacy.'

Even the valuable and interesting newscasts have a minus as well as a plus. Newsman John Chancellor pointed out that the difference between viewing TV newscasts and reading a newspaper is enormous. A man reading his newspaper can be his own editor. But with TV, you have either to take it, or turn it off.

So, even after making generous allowance for the undoubted beneficial aspects of TV, it must be said that it is responsible for a growing degree of isolation and consequent loneliness, even within the family.

But one can be very lonely even in the midst of the family circle. The sharp increase reported in family violence indicates that there is significantly less wholesome communication, but more isolation and estrangement, than in former days. Then, it was the family that provided stability and afforded the basic environment for the normal development of personality. Now, on the contrary, violence within the family is emerging as a major source of crime. Refuges for battered wives and children have become the order of the day.

It is reported that 20 per cent of police deaths in the USA is attributed to police intervention in family disputes. The ultimate effect of this violence on the children, who learn their behaviour patterns in the home, is to perpetuate those patterns in the homes of the next generation. This is not theory but established fact.

One would have expected the home to be the place of deepest intimacy—and in many cases it is. But too often it has degenerated into a place of shattered ideals and blasted hopes. Instead of love, there are loneliness and isolation. As one writer put it: 'More people are feeling lonely, their lives consist of proximity without presence, relationship without contact, and familiarity without feelings.'[1]

One hopeful sign in an otherwise bleak picture is the increased attention being paid by both church and state to the importance of the family in the life of the nation. In both circles, increasing numbers of well-qualified and caring professional people are being assigned to work in this vastly important segment of the community.

5

LONELINESS AFFECTS HEALTH

'A nine-year study by researchers at the University of California shows that loneliness has greater impact on the death rate than smoking, drinking, eating or exercise. The study found that people without spouses or friends had a death rate twice as high as those with social ties.'[1]

Loneliness is usually considered to be mainly a matter of the emotions, and indeed it is. But in its acute and unrelieved form its effects are not confined to the emotions. Specialists in the sphere of mental and emotional health assert that it can induce most painful and even harmful physical repercussions, as many a sufferer has learned to his dismay.

For this reason, if for no other, it must be viewed as a serious health hazard. One eminent specialist advanced the opinion that there is a biological basis for our need to form close human relationships, and added that if we fail to do this we are putting our health at risk. So it is a matter of urgency that the lonely person diligently endeavours to analyse its cause in his or her case, and seeks the appropriate remedy.

The physiological effects vary with the individual, since the constitution of each person is unique. Migraine, exhaustion or listlessness are common side-effects. Eating habits may be affected, or obesity as a result of over-eating in the search for some compensating influence for the inner ache. In some cases sexual desire is totally inhibited or greatly decreased. If the lonely condition is unduly prolonged or excessive in degree, it has been known to produce a significant change in personality.

Profound psychological effects may be induced. Since emotion plays such a dominant role in the whole of life, undue suppression of the emotions, or a conscious effort to suppress them, can have harmful psychological repercussions. The better course is to find some satisfying outlet for them— even tears—than to keep them suppressed. The macho image that some men try to display can be seriously counter-productive in this respect.

It is an understandable though inverted tendency on the part of lonely persons to take refuge in withdrawing into themselves, rather than seeking the company of others. This reaction often has its rise in a fear that in any close relationship some failure or other personality defect may surface, bringing it to an untimely end. Although they are all the time craving friendship, this fear causes them to keep their true self concealed. This, in turn, renders it difficult for them to make the first approach and equally difficult for others to make a friendly advance.

The prominent psychiatrist, William Glasser, makes this surprising assertion: 'All symptoms, whether psychological or psychosomatic, and all aggressive, irrational behaviour, are products of loneliness, and are companions to the lonely, suffering people who struggle for an identity, but do not succeed. Instead, they identify themselves as failures.'[2]

No less serious are the inroads made on family life. The absence of stable foundations for family life creates an atmosphere of insecurity and uncertainty that only worsens the condition. With a minority it causes them to lash out in violent speech or action. Rather than becoming depressed as do others in like case, they get angry and express their frustrations in destructive activity. May not this be a major cause of the unprecedented outbreaks of violent crime that plague our cities today?

Alcohol and drug addiction are often symptoms of this endemic loneliness. But they are not the real malady. When a lonely person fails to find acceptance in normal society, he or she may try this escape route which at first promises so much, but in the end delivers so little and ends in a depressing cul-de-sac.

Then, too, there is a vital connection between loneliness and sickness. People overtaken by serious illness are of necessity compelled to spend much time alone. Usually they are taken by surprise when such a visitation overtakes them, and are therefore unprepared to meet the crisis. The stark contrast between the liberty enjoyed by friends and loved ones, and their own severance from the normal pursuits of life, is often a painful experience.

If the sick person is confined to a hospital or nursing home, visiting hours are limited and, even where they are more generous, friends do not have unlimited time for visitation. When loneliness is added to the pain incidental to the illness, they can weigh on the spirits of even the most buoyant patient.

Hospital chaplains report that in the course of their visitation they meet many patients who have no friends, no one to visit and cheer them from year to year. To such sufferers loneliness is inevitable and corrosive. It is small wonder if their thoughts turn inwards in self-pity and they succumb to bitterness.

Chronic illness and infirmity always lead to a measure of isolation. With the passage of time, friends move away or drop off for one reason or another. In larger cities the distances to be traversed are another limiting factor. So visitors become less frequent.

One survey of homes for the aged uncovered the disturbing fact that 70 per cent of the residents had not had a single visitor the previous year. Slowly they had become forgotten or neglected. The intensity of the loneliness of these people is not difficult to imagine.

But there is no need for a sick-bed to become a prison. It is possible for our minds and imaginations to people our solitude. The Christian who knows 'the comfort of the Scriptures,' and who maintains a vital and outgoing prayer-life, will find in those exercises a satisfying panacea for his own need. He can rove the world in his prayers and thus contribute to the fulfilment of Christ's great commission.

A glowing example of one who rose above her confining surroundings is that of Madame Jeanne de la Mothe Guyon, a member of the French nobility who, during the French Revolution, was imprisoned in the infamous Bastille for 15 years.

In spite of the atrocious conditions in which she found herself, so great was her delight in God that her spirit soared far above her prison walls. She said the stones in her prison walls shone like rubies. Triumphant in spirit, she penned these verses:

> *'A little bird am I.*
> *Shut out from fields of air,*
> *Yet in my cage I sit and sing*
> *To Him who placed me there!*
> *Well pleased a prisoner to be,*
> *Because, my God, it pleaseth Thee.*
>
> *Naught else have I to do,*
> *I sing the whole day long,*
> *And He whom most I love to please*
> *Doth listen to my song.*
> *He caught and bound my wandering wing,*
> *And still He loves to hear me sing.*
>
> *My cage confines me round,*
> *Abroad I cannot soar,*
> *But though my wing is closely bound*
> *My heart's at liberty.*
> *My prison walls cannot control*
> *The flight, the freedom of the soul.*

O it is good to soar
These bolts and bars above,
To Him whose purpose I adore,
Whose providence I love,
    And in Thy mighty will to find
    The joy and freedom of the mind.'

Like that confining prison, a sickbed can be transformed into a throne and become a centre of ministry and salvation, as the following incident reveals:

In 1939 it was my privilege to visit one of God's great noblewomen, Hannah R. Higgens of Melbourne, Australia. For 69 of her 82 years she had been in constant pain as the result of a progressive bone disease which necessitated the ultimate amputation of both arms and legs. 'Yet in her little cage she sat and sang to Him who placed her there.' She named her cottage 'Gladwish'. For 43 years she lived in one room.

How easy it would have been for her to give up the struggle and relapse into an orgy of self-pity. Instead, she accepted her limitations and took as her God-given ministry the sharing with other invalids the love and comfort of God that had been her portion.

She had an attachment fixed to the stump of her right arm which enabled her to write with a fountain pen. It takes little imagination to conceive the physical effort involved in writing, since she had to use her whole body to form the letters. As I write, I have before me one of her letters in the almost copperplate script she learned to write.

That little room became a place of pilgrimage for

people from all over the world. From it went thousands of letters to visitors and fellow-sufferers worldwide, which produced a rich harvest of blessing. The walls of her room were covered with photographs of correspondents to whom she had ministered and in many cases had led to the Lord. Of her it could be truly said that she turned her trouble into treasure and her sorrow into song.

> 'I have so much to be thankful for, so many mercies,' she wrote. 'I have often tried to count them but it is impossible. They are innumerable. Although I am deprived of health and strength and my limbs, Jesus is far more precious than ever . . . I am so often asked if I do not find the time long, *I do not, and I can truthfully say that I never feel lonely.*'[3]

Who can measure the glory and joy this valiant sufferer brought to the heart of God, or the streams of blessing that flowed around the world from that humble room?

As I write, I have received a letter from a friend in which he says: 'While walking in the desert, Moses discovered a bush on fire. Amazingly, the bush was not burning up, so Moses drew closer to see why. Then God spoke to him out of the burning bush.

'It was not unusual to see a bush burning; it is unusual that the bush was not consumed. It's not unusual to see people hit by fiery trials; it's remarkable when they are not consumed by them. *And*

God often speaks to onlookers through one in the midst of trial.'

6

SINGLE, YET NOT LONELY

'I live alone, and yet I am never lonely. Why should I be lonely when I have God?' These words were spoken by a woman 90 years old, in precarious health and with few worldly goods, whom I visited recently. She exemplified the fact that singleness need not be equated with loneliness.

Each generation evolves its own name for different categories of people. 'Teenagers' and 'yuppies' are 'in' words today. But in this half of the 20th century a new grouping has emerged—'singles' and 'solo parents.' Of course they have always been with us, but never in the proportions they have reached today. Either by choice or by force of circumstances, an increasing number are living alone.

The prevalence of divorce and acceptance of homosexuality as an alternative lifestyle have added dramatically to their numbers. So significant is this shift in our culture that it has disturbed the whole social structure and necessitated major changes in legislation.

The emergence of a high-technology society and the pressures of financial need have influenced more women to focus on their careers, rather than on home and family as formerly. The comparative affluence enjoyed in many western lands tends to encourage the growth of the single lifestyle. Considerable numbers are opting out of entering into a marriage contract and just live together.

It is reported that the number of American citizens living alone increased by 385 per cent between the years 1971—1981. The corollary is that the number of children living with solo parents has also greatly increased. Almost one person in three lives alone. A comparable trend, although to a somewhat lesser extent, is occurring in other developed lands.

The single woman is especially prone to suffer from acute loneliness as she sees her peers marrying and establishing homes and families of their own. Many yearn deeply for the fulfilment of their God-given capacity for motherhood. In a world that is geared largely to the married, she is tempted to feel a misfit and not desirable. But our society is adapting to this situation.

SINGLENESS AND MISSIONS

When thinking of singleness, however, we should not overlook the fact that Jesus and Paul found satisfaction and fulfilment in the single state. Some of the world's greatest saints, both men and women, have been single.

The mission-fields of the world would be greatly denuded were it not for the magnificent contribution of single women—a contribution that fortunately continues.

A striking example of the way in which a group of

single women found fulfilment in their single state, occurred in the interior of China. J. Hudson Taylor, founder of the China Inland Mission (now Overseas Missionary Fellowship), was a pioneer in several areas of missionary work. It was he who first encouraged lay persons to undertake missionary work. It was he, too, who first engaged single women in pioneering new areas in China. In 1885 the Mission opened centres on the populous Kwang Sin River, and because there were no men available for the task, the work was conducted entirely by single women.

Thirty-two years later there was a complete chain of 10 central stations, 60 outstations, over 2,000 communicants, and large numbers of inquirers, pupils in schools, etc. These and other single women who joined them were still the only foreign missionaries alongside the national pastors they had trained. No one could say that they had not found fulfilment, even though single.

PAUL'S VIEWPOINT

In his classic treatment of the subject of the unmarried or the widowed, Paul, writing by inspiration, three times repeated the assertion, 'it is good to be (or remain) unmarried.' Nothing either the Lord or Paul said on the subject would give rise to the idea that to be single constituted one a second-class person or Christian. Here are his statements:

'*It is good* for a man not to marry' (1 Cor 7.1).

'Now to the unmarried and the widows I say: *It is good* for them to stay unmarried, as I am' (1 Cor 7.8).

'Now about the virgins, I have no command-
ment from the Lord, but I give my judgment
. . . *Because of the present crisis,* I think *it is
good* for you to remain as you are . . .

Are you unmarried? Do not seek for a wife' (1
Cor 7.25, 26: *italics mine*).

In the first two verses Paul makes it clear that he
is writing by command of the Lord. In the third
passage he states that it is an expression of his sanc-
tified judgment concerning the wisdom or otherwise of getting married, *in view of the current critical
political situation.* He is not laying down a universal
prohibition for all time.

He does not indicate the nature of the crisis but,
in those turbulent days in the Roman Empire,
crises were common. He apparently considered the
existing crisis so serious as to believe that the wiser
course for the unmarried would be to remain single
until the crisis was resolved.

CHRIST'S TEACHING
Our Lord, too, made an important pronouncement
on the subject, which gives assurance that singleness can be both honourable and praiseworthy:

'There are some eunuchs who were so
born from their mother's womb; and
there are eunuchs who were made
eunuchs by men; and there are
eunuchs who have made themselves
eunuchs for the Kingdom of heaven's
sake. He that is able to receive it, let

him receive it' (Mt 19.12).

The implication is plain. There are some who are so disciplined and motivated as to be able to, and who do, choose singleness in order that they may better give undistracted service to the Lord and their fellow men. History is replete with glorious examples of such people.

Jesus did not make this mandatory, but optional. Not everyone can rise to such a disciplined lifestyle. But it must be acknowledged that the Church and the world owe much to those who have deliberately chosen this sacrificial course.

So, from the teaching of both Christ and Paul, we learn that neither regarded the single state as a second-best. Nor should single people consider themselves in any sense inferior or under-privileged. Paul reinforced this view when he wrote:

> 'I wish all men were as I am. But each
> man has his own gift from God; one
> man has this gift'—the gift of being
> married—'and another that'—the gift
> of being single (1 Cor 7.7).

But not all single people are able to regard their state in that light! It is not unnatural for them to compare their lot with that of their contemporaries who, after work, return to a welcoming home and family, and not to an empty apartment.

Sometimes circumstances make it either inadvisable or impossible to marry. For others the opportunity of marriage has not come their way; or a promising relationship has not materialised. In such

cases, the well-worn but oft-proved saying stands
true—'In *acceptance lies peace.*' The converse is
equally true.

On one occasion the author heard a single
missionary in her early thirties give her testimony
before leaving for her second furlough. She told
frankly of her longing for a life-partner, and admitted what a struggle it had been for her to face
the continuing loneliness of single life on the
mission-field.

So when furlough time came round, she decided
that she must realistically face and settle the matter
once and for all. She said to herself: 'Well, it appears
you're 'on the shelf.' No one seems to be dying to
marry you, in spite of your prayers. You might as
well accept that as final and get on with your job.'

Once she had definitely faced and accepted the
fact of her singleness as being God's good and perfect will for her, the tumult subsided and her heart
was at peace. She testified that she was going home
full of joy and peace, even though she was per-
manently 'on the shelf.'

But that was not the end of the story. Not long
after her return to the field, to her joy and surprise
she discovered that someone *was* 'dying to marry
her.' Today she and her husband are making a valuable contribution to the Kingdom of God in Asia.

It must be admitted that things do not always
work out so happily, but the point to observe is that
once she had accepted the fact of her singleness,
instead of rebelling and fighting against it, the dove
of peace alighted on her heart. But even if no offer
of marriage had come to her, the peace of God
would have ousted the old loneliness, and she

would have proved the truth of Paul's assertion that 'the will of God is good, acceptable and perfect.' She would be able to sing with Tersteegen:

> *'Thou sweet, beloved will of God,*
> *My anchor ground, my fortress hill,*
> *My spirit's silent, fair abode,*
> *In Thee I hide me and am still.*
>
> *Upon God's will I lay me down,*
> *As child upon its mother's breast;*
> *No silken couch, nor softest bed*
> *Could ever give me such deep rest.*
>
> *Thy wonderful, grand will, my God,*
> *With triumph now I make it mine,*
> *And faith shall cry a joyous, Yes!*
> *To every dear command of Thine.'*

SINGLENESS HAS SOME ADVANTAGES

This is another angle that should be taken into consideration. With so many marriages ending in the divorce court, the loneliness which engulfs the parties to these broken marriages is probably more acute than that of the unmarried person. For the divorcee there are in addition a host of complicating factors, especially where children are involved. 'Single bliss can be preferable to marital misery.'

It was usually thought and taught that the married state was God's ideal for men and women, and there is no question that it is the normal state. But in our contemporary world this ideal cannot be realised, because there are not enough men to go round! Inevitably some women must remain single.

If the single state is God's will for some, both men and women, even though marriage might be preferred, that will nevertheless is 'good, acceptable and perfect.' The converse is also true—anything other than the will of God is bad, unacceptable and imperfect. Because it is acceptable, it should be accepted, adapted to, and adorned.

Philip the evangelist was blessed with four unmarried daughters (Ac 21.8, 9). Their singleness did not prevent their being prophetesses and exercising a fruitful and satisfying ministry. They were highly esteemed in the Early Church. Indeed, in writing of them, Eusebius, one of the Church Fathers, described them as 'mighty luminaries in the Early Church.'

This should surely encourage other single women who are not sure of their status in Christian work. Their ministry was much more than getting cups of tea for the men. Down the centuries devoted single women have had a similar invaluable ministry. It is said of Henrietta Mears of California, for example, that her ministry and personal interest was a dominant factor in the lives of one hundred of America's great Christian leaders.

Single women are free to establish close ties with other single people of all ages, as well as with families. She has abundant scope for her home-making instincts and exercising her aesthetic tastes. She can extend imaginative hospitality to the lonely and homeless. If she has her own home, it can be used in the interests of the Kingdom.

Although they have no children of their own, single women have love to give away, and they can lavish their affection on other people's children.

And when affection is given, it is usually reciprocated.

A missionary who was nearing the 70 mark once said to the author: 'Do you know one of the first questions I am going to ask the Lord when I get to heaven?'

'No,' I replied.

'I am going to ask Him why He didn't give me a husband. I wanted a husband badly, and I would have made him a good wife!'

By now she will have had her answer! God's denial did not sour her or make her resentful and bitter, however. Instead, she poured the wealth of affection she would have lavished on her husband and family into the lives of thousands of children in China and Britain, for the Lord gave her a unique ministry to children.

When she was called home a few years ago, there would be hundreds on the other side, waiting to welcome her. She found heart-rest in accepting the Lord's assurance—'You do not realise now what I am doing, but later you will understand' (Jn 13.7).

So singleness can be activated for God and made spiritually productive. Blessing comes more by giving than by receiving. Remember the ninth beatitude: 'It is more blessed to give than to receive' (Ac 20.35).

The source from which the Lord drew comfort in His days on earth is open to all:

> 'A time is coming, and has come, when you will be scattered, each to his own home. *You will leave me all alone. Yet I am not alone, for the Father is with me*' (Jn 16.32: *italics mine*).

7

THE DESOLATION OF BEREAVEMENT

One of the most prolific creators of loneliness and a
sense of desolation, is the natural grief and sorrow
that accompany bereavement. In the early stages of
that shattering experience, the sense of loss of the
loved one is so all-pervasive that the bereaved
person cannot believe the sun will ever shine again.
It seems quite outside the bounds of possibility that
one could ever again face life with any semblance of
enjoyment.

Elisabeth Elliott, as she was when her husband
was murdered by the Auca Indians of Latin America,
to whom he and his four fellow-missionaries had
gone with the gospel, describes in poignant words
her earliest reactions to the unexpected experience
of bereavement. The sentiments she expresses will
have a familiar ring to those of us who have trodden
the same path:

> 'Silent, swift, implacable, the Scythe
> has swept by, and we are left . . . The
> mail comes, the phone rings, Wednes-
> day gives place to Thursday, and this

week to next week.
'You have to keep on getting up in the
morning and comb your hair (for
whom?), eating breakfast (remember
to get out only one egg now), making
the bed (who cares?)'

The poignancy of the unaccustomed aloneness
lies in the absence of someone to love, care for, talk
things over with and to serve. Someone to join in
the decision-making process; someone with whom
to share life's joys and laughter, life's pains and
sorrows. Someone with whom to revel in new and
exciting discoveries in God's Word and God's
world. We sorrow alone, and are inclined to think,
mistakenly of course, that no one has felt or could
feel the intensity of the pangs of loneliness and
sorrow as we do.

In the aftermath of the homecall of his dearly
loved wife, Sarah, the veteran Southern preacher
Vance Havner wrote these words, which will strike
a responsive chord in the hearts of those recently
bereaved:

'Again and again I find myself saying,
"Sarah is gone!" Gone with her are a
thousand other precious things that
made the past so delightful. Gone is
the anticipation of returning home to
be greeted at the apartment door, or
at the airport. Gone is the thrill of
hearing her voice at the other end of
the telephone, and the cheery, "Hey,
honey!"

Gone are those daily airmail letters in the mail box . . . Gone is that lovely face in the congregation, smiling at jokes she has heard me tell countless times. Gone—and the chilling, numbing awareness that it can never be again. All these years I have travelled, but never has loneliness descended on me as now. I find myself instinctively, subconsciously, looking around as though my dear Sarah ought to be somewhere nearby, reading a magazine, just waiting to be happy with me. I miss her dreadfully, but I cannot wish her back. Rather, I mend my step, and hasten on to overtake her.'[1]

GRIEF SHOULD BE ACCEPTED AND EXPRESSED

Sooner or later grief must be accepted as an inevitable part of the human situation. We must face realistically the fact that, in the ordinary course of events, one partner in every marriage can expect to travel the last lap of the race alone. Some of our contemporaries will predecease us. But the clock of life does not stop with the death of a loved partner or friend—it must go on, and so must we.

> *'Life must go on*
> *And the dead be forgotten;*
> *Life must go on*
> *Though good men die;*
> *Anne, eat your breakfast;*
> *Dan, take your medicine!*

THE DESOLATION OF BEREAVEMENT

Life must go on,
I just forget why.'

Edna St. Vincent Millay

The important fact is, however, that we can and do choose the manner in which we finish our own race. We are not the playthings of an inexorable Fate.

'Sorrow does colour life, doesn't it?' said a friend to another who had recently suffered bereavement.

'Yes, indeed it does,' was the reply, *'but I intend to choose the colours.'* What colours are we going to choose?

The author recently received a letter from a friend who had lost his wife. It was written in the early stages of his grief. '"Oh for the touch of a vanished hand, and the sound of a voice that is still" is a quotation that had little significance for me until the finger of God touched my dear wife. I was left in the desolation and silence of living alone. However there is no cessation from living, despite the changed conditions and the altered rhythm to which it is hard to adjust. "My grace is sufficient" is a precious promise that enables one to go on.'

'Let sorrow do its work,
   Come grief or pain
Sweet are thy messengers,
   Sweet their refrain;
When they can sing with me
   More love O Christ to Thee,
    More love to Thee.'

Elizabeth Prentiss

In the early stages of bereavement, although we may be familiar with the book answers and the prescriptions tendered by loving friends for the alleviation of our grief, while we may give intellectual assent to well-meant assurances that time will heal the ache, our emotions strenuously deny any such possibility. The tendency is to search for some immediate escape route.

'Some people run away from grief, go on world cruises, or move to another town. But they do not escape, I think. The memories unbidden spring into their minds, scattered perhaps over the years. *There is something to be said for facing them all deliberately, and straightaway.*'[2]

But as one who has twice suffered the trauma of parting with a dearly-loved wife, the author can say out of his own experience that while time does not and cannot remove the deep sense of loss, it does blunt the sharp edge of sorrow.

At times a sense of desolation will sweep over one, but these onslaughts diminish in frequency with the passage of time. If then with firm purpose we turn our thoughts away from ourselves towards meeting the needs of others, it is remarkable how our own grief is assuaged.

There is a limited sense in which time is the great healer and consoler, but as will be shown later, it is God, our loving Father, who holds that office, for He is 'the Father of compassion, and the God of all comfort, who comforts us in all our troubles' (2 Cor 1.3, 4). 'We should never lose sight of the fact that in the desert of our sorrow, there is the refreshing well of the comfort of God.'

Was is not predicted of the coming Messiah that

the Lord would send him

> *'to bind up the broken-hearted . . . to comfort all who mourn, and provide for those who grieve* in Zion—to bestow on them a crown of beauty instead of ashes, the oil of gladness instead of mourning, and a garment of praise instead of despair'* (Is 61.1–3: *italics mine*).

We must never underestimate what God can do for us in these circumstances, even though at the time the thought of receiving comfort seems a very remote possibility. He is 'able to do exceedingly abundantly, above all we ask or think.'

In his classic, *David Copperfield,* Charles Dickens depicts Mrs Gummidge as the most utterly selfish and bad-tempered woman in Yarmouth. But when the town was caught up in a great disaster, she forgot herself in ministering to her needy neighbours in their distress. The experience transformed her. Copperfield was astounded at the unbelievable transformation in her character. Far from being self-centred, she now became a self-forgetful servant of the community. Dickens was a very discerning psychologist. Loneliness and self-forgetfulness cannot sleep in the same bed.

CHRISTIANS SORROW, BUT NOT AS OTHERS

It is possible for us to become so obsessed with our loss that we become overwhelmed with excessive grief. While giving expression to our grief openly, rather than suppressing it, is beneficial and necessary, there can be an excess of grief that is damaging both psychologically and spiritually. And more important still, it is dishonouring to our loving, caring, heavenly Father. It is right for Christians to sorrow as other men and women do, for being a Christian does not de-humanise one. But they should not sorrow in the same way as those who have no hope beyond the grave.

The attitude of a Christian to the homecall of a loved one must seem paradoxical to those who have no personal experience of the love and care of our Father in heaven, and do not share the hope He gives of a joyous reunion beyond the grave.

To most non-Christians, death is an unmitigated tragedy to be postponed for as long as possible. In the death of a believer there is a marked difference. The sorrow of those left behind is no less real and painful, but there are compensating factors which God brings into play, that kindle hope through tears and shed light amid the gloom.

Who that cares for the loved departed can keep on grieving that their loved one has been released from the trammels of an ailing body and is now in the immediate presence of Christ, which Paul assures us is 'far better'? To enjoy unending union with Him and revel in the communion of the saints, is no cause for sorrow. The symbolism in a Salvation Army funeral, in which the dominant colour is white, is nearer the outlook of the New Testament than the traditional black of hopeless mourning.

While not a sure-fire cure for sorrow, concentration on these positive aspects surrounding the loss of a loved one will in some measure help to counteract an excessive dwelling upon our own sense of loss.

Hugging our sorrow, continuing to fuel our grief, will only perpetuate the pain and render it yet more difficult for us to recapture a semblance of normal life and usefulness in the community. We should not try to keep our grief alive, as do some who shrink from the thought that life can again return to near normalcy. To succumb to this view of things will make us the prisoner of our sorrow and prevent us from reaching out to fresh and stimulating goals in the days ahead.

> 'Brothers, we do not want you to be ignorant about those who fall asleep, *or to grieve like the rest of men, who have no hope.* We believe that Jesus died and rose again, and so we believe that God will bring with Jesus those who have fallen asleep in him.' (1 Thes 4.13, 14: *italics mine*).

Bishop Frank Houghton, the author's predecessor as General Director of the China Inland Mission (now Overseas Missionary Fellowship), displayed a mature attitude to the death of his younger sister, to whom he was very attached. In writing to his friend Amy W. Carmichael, founder of the Dohnavur Fellowship in India, he said:

> *'Many of our friends in their letters of sympathy speak of God's mysterious ways, and I know there is an element of mystery. But I shrink from the*

suggestion that our Father has done anything that needs to be explained. What He has done is the best, because He has done it, and I pray that as a family we may not cast about for explanation, but exult in the Holy Spirit and say, "I thank thee, Father . . . Even so Father . . ." It suggests a lack of confidence in Him if we find it necessary to understand all He does. Will it not bring greater joy to tell Him that we need no explanation because we know Him? "As for God, his way is perfect," said the psalmist. If His way is perfect we need no explanation.'

*'We may not see just here and now
With vision clear the why and how
Of all that God seems to allow,
    But "afterward" . . .'*

Josephine Butler, a noted British social worker of a former day, proved in a dramatic manner that one way to relieve one's own burden of sorrow is to shoulder that of someone else.

On coming home one day, her little daughter ran out of an upstairs room to greet her. She leaned over the balustrade to see her mother, overbalanced and crashed to the ground. The mother was broken-hearted, but the God of all comfort did not fail her in her distress.

An older Quaker lady came to comfort her, and said, 'I have spent most of my life looking after girls from the streets. I am old now and I can no longer handle the work of looking after the home where 40 of them live. Come and take my job, and you will forget your sorrow.'

Josephine took over the care of the home and found great fulfilment in doing so. While, of course, she never really forgot her sorrow, by taking on her shoulders the troubles and cares of others, she discovered a panacea for her own loss.

> 'Seldom can a heart be lonely
> If it seeks a lonelier still,
> Self-forgetful, longing only
> Emptier cups to fill.'
>
> Eleanor Standinmeyer

8

GOD CARES FOR THE WIDOWED

'In loving, you and I assume the risk
of loss . . . We're so happy now, but
we must accept the fact that one of us
will have to live without the other
some day.'[1]

Helen Raley

From whatever point of view it is approached, the
lot of the widow—or widower—is anything but en-
viable. Theirs is essentially a lonely sorrow that in
most cases is not easily assuaged.

All married couples, if they are realists, must
sooner or later face the fact, inevitably, in the course
of time one or other of them will be confronted with
the necessity of walking the remaining pathway of
life alone. Statistics tell us that it is much more
likely to be the wife who survives. Increasingly, the
life expectancy of women continues to outstrip that
of men. It is not morbid to face this incontrovertible
reality. Rather is it the part of wisdom, for too
many spouses have had to meet the dreaded crisis
unprepared.

One recently bereaved wife whose husband had been ill for a considerable time, told of her reaction when at last he was taken from her. 'Though I had lived with Walter's illness for several years, steeling myself for the eventuality of his death,' she confessed, 'I found myself as unprepared as a passenger in a boat who is suddenly dumped into the water. I realise now that this state of blank bewilderment is fairly normal for anyone moving through the grief process.'[2]

Perhaps some starkly realistic forethought and planning might have greatly reduced the trauma of the experience and its inevitable accompaniments.

But no matter how carefully we may have conditioned ourselves for the possible passing of our partner, or how realistically we may have prepared ourselves in mind for the actual transition, inevitably there comes the shock and the grim reality of the final parting. Its effects can be overwhelming. Not infrequently, for a time it saps the very will to live through the bleakness of the widowed state.

When we are in the early stages of grief that sweep over one, some well-meaning friend will assure us that time is a great healer. But at the time it seems only another empty cliché, utterly divorced from reality. It may be true in the case of others, but it could not be in our case.

The dark reality, that cannot be evaded, is that the loved one is no longer there to love and be loved. A companionship that has grown dearer and deeper with the years is not readily replaced, nor is the aching void speedily filled.

It was Søren Kierkegaard's contention that suffering is incommunicable. There is also a very real sense in which the suffering and loneliness of the widowed, too, is incommunicable and must be borne alone.

> *'There is a mystery of human hearts,*
> *And though encircled by a host*
> *Of those who love us well, and are*
> *beloved,*
> *To every one of us from time to time*
> *There comes a sense of utter lonelines.*
>
> *Our dearest friend is stranger to our*
> *joy,*
> *And cannot realise our bitterness.*
> *"There is not one who really under-*
> *stands,*
> *No one to enter in to what I feel."*
> *Such is the cry of each of us in turn.*
>
> *We wander in a solitary way,*
> *No matter what our lot may be;*
> *Each heart, mysterious even to itself,*
> *Must live its inner life in solitude.'*

These poignant lines portray the experience of most of us. But for the Christian, while the sense of loss is no less real, there is a compensating factor which is not mentioned in the poem—the realised, comforting presence of the God of all comfort.

> 'Praise be to the God and Father of
> our Lord Jesus Christ, the Father of
> compassion and the God of all com-
> fort, who comforts us in all our

78

troubles, so that we can comfort
those in any trouble with the comfort
we ourselves have received from God.'
(2 Cor 1.3, 4)

In the early days of their bereavement, widows
and widowers—I speak from experience—receive a
great deal of sympathy and support from relatives
and friends who are genuinely concerned to alleviate
in some measure the grief of those they love. They
receive many invitations out to meals and other
social occasions. Friends drop in for a chat now and
again. But amid the hectic pressures of the space
age, the demands of life are so great that almost
inevitably the number of visitors declines and invitations out become fewer. It is not that our friends
have ceased caring, but there is a limit to what can
be crowded into one day.

'In a society that is couples-orientated
as ours is, the single person is sometimes viewed as a social embarrassment
whom it is not easy to fit into the picture. Our society is also sex-orientated,
and the accepted standard in social life
is the couple. Whether justified or not,
single women tend to feel that society
does not fully accept or make room for
the single woman, whether that status
is voluntary or not. This is in part the
reason for the proliferation of singles
groups in churches. Unfortunately
such people often find that they must
live on the periphery of society—out of

the mainstream.'

When it has been the husband who has been popular and the life of the party, the problem is even more acute. A friend recently told the author of his daughter and her husband who moved to another city. They purchased a home in a new suburb where few of the houses were completed. Consequently there were few near neighbours, and they had not been sufficiently long in the community to establish close relationships.

When, as the result of an accident, her husband was killed, the widow was left alone with two little children. Most of the acquaintances they had made were friends of the husband rather than of her own making. Suddenly she found herself bereaved, living in a sparsely inhabited neighbourhood, in a strange city with few friends; all alone with her grief and facing a desolate future. In our great cities similar tragic situations can be multiplied a hundredfold.

It is sometimes assumed or suggested that the lot of the widower is less distressing than that of the widow. This is doubtless true in many cases, but in our contemporary society, though the plight of the widower is no less acute, it attracts much less concern.

In the anguish of his unexpected bereavement, C.S. Lewis penned these words: 'Oh God, why did you take so much trouble to force this creature out of its shell, if it is now doomed to crawl back—to be sucked back—into it?'[3]

Not infrequently, a widower is much more poorly equipped to handle the changed circumstances than is his feminine counterpart. This is especially so if he is not somewhat domesticated. The situation becomes even more complicated and stressful when children are left in his care. He feels at a desperate disadvantage, and life can become a harrowing experience when this responsibility is added to the burden of his grief.

Perhaps out of his own experience Alfred Lord Tennyson wrote:

> *'Tears of a widower when he sees*
> *A late lost form that sleep reveals,*
> *And moves his doubtful arms and feels*
> *Her place is empty—fall like these.'*

The wife of the author's second marriage, who is now with the Lord, had been a widow for a number of years. She had felt the loneliness of widowhood very keenly. If she went out in the evening to attend a meeting or social function, she found returning to the lonely house a daunting and desolating experience, the poignancy of which did not fade with the passing years.

Lord Byron knew something of the same emotion:

> *''Tis sweet to hear the watchdog's bark*
> *Bay deep-mouthed welcome as we draw near home;*
> *'Tis sweet to know there is an eye will mark*
> *Our coming, and will look brighter when we come.'*

Although it is probably without full justification,

many widows feel that there is somehow a stigma attaching to widowhood that exacerbates its inevitable loneliness. Whether this is real or imagined is immaterial, for there is abundant testimony that the feeling is nonetheless there.

In writing of her reactions after her famous husband's death, Helen Raley made this observation: 'I was to learn that although widowhood presents a woman sometimes as a non-person or a half-person, she need not succumb to the hopeless abandonment of life. Nor need she forget, for any reason, the identity she once shared with her husband. Awareness of this is a way towards self-hood, a disciplined motivation and a measure of contentment . . . For the survivor, life must go on. The death of a loved one does not mean the end of all things, and somehow, sooner or later, reality must be faced.'[4]

THE BIBLICAL OUTLOOK

It must be admitted that in our western society there is a tendency, not always conscious or intentional, to neglect or even ostracise widows. This was not the case in Old Testament times. God ordained that special provision be made for them, and He expressed His concern lest they be exploited:

> 'Do not take advantage of a widow. If you do, and they cry out to me, I will certainly hear their cry. My anger will be aroused' (Ex 22.22, 23).

In instructing the Israelites concerning their behaviour when they entered on their inheritance in Canaan, God, through Moses, gave further expression of His concern:

> 'Do not take the cloak of a widow as a
> pledge . . . When you are harvesting
> your field and you overlook a sheaf,
> do not go back to get it. Leave it for
> the alien, the fatherless and the
> widow' (Dt 24.17–19).

A similar charitable attitude was to be observed when they were harvesting grapes and olives. The charming biblical story of Ruth illustrates the manner in which this instruction was carried out by the caring Israelite.

The New Testament is no less solicitous for the plight of the widow. Acts 6.1–3 shows how the apostles viewed and handled this situation in the earliest days of the church. The Hellenistic Jews lodged a complaint with the apostles that their widows were being overlooked in the daily distribution of relief. The apostles immediately demonstrated their concern that the widows should receive equitable treatment. Seven men of ability and integrity were selected by the church to oversee this worthy social service.

Both Paul and James challenged the churches to which they wrote, to act responsibly towards the widows in their midst.

The psalmist had a true conception of the God of the widow when he wrote:

> 'A father to the fatherless, a defender
> of the widows, is God in his holy
> dwelling' (Ps 68.5).

PRACTICAL PROBLEMS

Many married women have left financial and business affairs entirely to their husbands. When they are widowed they feel lost and unable to handle these responsibilities by themselves. After a life of shared decision-making, it is a shock to have to make them alone. Of course it is wisdom to consult competent friends or counsellors, but the final decision is one's own and must be taken, for once made one has to live with it.

It is generally agreed that it is not wise for a widow to make far-reaching decisions too soon after the bereavement, when still in a state of deep shock. Acting precipitately may bring later regrets. When decisions have to be made, James's counsel should be acted upon:

> 'If any of you lacks wisdom'—and who does not?—'he should ask of God who gives generously to all without finding fault, and it will be given to him' (Jas 1.5).

Here is a definite undertaking by God that He will impart wisdom in decision-making to the one who asks for it. It is a promise to be believed, appropriated and acted on.

With this assurance, and the facts of the case before us, we can confidently trust Him to guide us in our mental processes as we weigh up the pros and cons. But knowing how easy it is to yield to unbelief, James adds a caution:

> 'But when he asks, he must believe
> and not doubt, because he who
> doubts is like a wave of the sea,
> blown and tossed by the wind. That
> man should not think he will receive
> anything from the Lord' (Jas 1.6, 7).

Some widows have always left driving the car to the husband, and when he is taken they are largely immobilised. A friend of the author who was in this position met the challenge of learning to drive, with determination and courage, although she was 74 years old. She passed the driving test on her first attempt. Now every time she takes her car out, she rejoices at the new mobility and freedom it has given. This may encourage another widow to make the attempt.

In his book, *Kathleen,* written shortly after his own bereavement, my friend of 60 years, Dr Edward M. Blaiklock, recorded this prayer which is especially appropriate for the widowed:

> *'Father, we pray for all lonely people,*
> *especially for those who, coming*
> *home to an empty house, stand at the*
> *door hesitant, afraid to enter. May all*
> *who stand in a doorway with fear in*
> *their hearts, like the two on the*
> *Emmaus road, ask the Living One*
> *in. Then, by His grace, may they find*
> *that in loneliness they are never alone,*
> *and that He peoples empty rooms with*
> *His presence.'*[5]

9

THE LONELINESS OF DIVORCE

While divorce may provide a solution for some marriage problems, it usually creates more complexities than it solves. It has been the experience of many that it can introduce one of the most desolate periods of life.

In the midst of the emotional turmoil which precipitates divorce, insufficient attention is likely to be paid to the far-reaching side consequences that will accrue. Only after the final break has taken place is the shattering discovery made that totally unexpected side-effects are involved. The parties had failed to face the implications realistically before the irrevocable step was taken.

> 'No one gets out completely unscarred,' writes Tim Stafford. 'When people who have grown together are separated, it's never a simple, clean disconnection. It's like pulling a tree out of the ground—it's a violent act, and you can't do it without some damage.'[1]

The soaring divorce rate the world around, an unhappy distinctive of our times, is inexorably creating an increasing community of the lonely. Especially in the affluent developed countries, with their plummeting moral standards, divorce has escalated at such a pace as to seriously threaten the very institution of marriage. The widening acceptance of homosexuality as an alternative lifestyle is accelerating the drift.

In my youth I did not know one divorced Christian. The case is far different today. In Britain, on present trends, one marriage in three will end in divorce. In the United States of America there is one divorce for every 1.8 marriages. (Happily, the latest figures indicate a slight decrease in the rate of divorce.) From 1960—1980 the number of divorced men and women more than tripled.[2] This means that divorce has now reached epidemic proportions and one serious consequence is, according to past experience, that what happens in America today will happen in other countries tomorrow. In Britain it is estimated that one child in five will experience the divorce of their parents before reaching the age of 16.

One survey revealed that only one third of American homes are made up of both parents and their children. Single family homes are increasing 20 times as fast as those of two-parent families. Real estate agents report that a great deal of the movement in the property market is a spin-off of this phenomenal rise in broken homes.

THE PLIGHT OF CHILDREN

The toll of emotional distress and insecurity that

this tragic development exacts from the children involved in these separations and divorces, hardly bears thinking about. Every lonely, unhappy person inevitably creates and diffuses an atmosphere of emotional tension and mute misery that soon spreads to others.

There is little doubt that the innocent children who are the victims of these fractured marriages suffer more severely than their parents, because they feel the consequent loss of love and security more severely than do mature adults. They become confused, because often they do not know to whom to turn for emotional help and support.

The resulting insecurity of this group spills over into their own subsequent marriage relationships. It is not surprising that many feel that if their parents' marriage ended in divorce, how can they feel secure in their own union? Divorce thus becomes a self-perpetuating agony. Much of the subsequent marriage break-up within this group can be traced back to the trauma caused by the divorce of their own parents.

Few children emerge from these family situations without deep emotional scars. A report in the *Journal of the Royal College of General Practitioners* of November 1986 showed that *pre-school* children were confused and frightened, and blamed themselves for the break-up. They expressed fears of being sent away from home.

School children expressed feelings of sadness and rejection, but did not normally blame themselves.

Children *over the age of nine* more often expressed anger and outrage at their parents' behaviour; they felt lonely and rejected. *Teenagers* also expressed these feelings and felt shame and embarrassment.

The divorce of parents caused more problems when it occurred before the children were five than when it happened later.

By *young adulthood* there was a higher incidence of illegitimate births, divorce, stomach ulcers and emotional problems.

In many cases of divorce it was the children and their future custody that lay at the heart of the marital quarrel, and this tends to generate in them an unwarranted sense of guilt. They feel that in some way they are to blame for the rupture.

One child psychologist maintains that the trauma consequent on divorce is second only to the death of a loved one, and this is especially the case with children. They become the subject of deep, inconsolable loss. When the familiar family structure collapses, the child is bewildered and feels lonely and frightened.

The children affected have to face many perplexing situations at an age when they are ill-equipped to cope with them. The question of loyalty arises. To which parent? They are pulled in both directions. They face the loss of one of their parents but, as often happens, through removal to another area, they may be parted from school and church friends as well. This can make very deep wounds that carry over into the future.

When parents are contemplating the possibility of divorce, in their preoccupation with the problems of their own relationships they do not always face sympathetically the consequences to the children of the marriage.

To incorporate a new father or mother into the

family structure is never an easy transition, and more often than not it produces adverse reactions on the part of the children.

DIVORCE LEADS TO CHRONIC LONELINESS

Both research and experience combine to predict that divorce is more likely to lead to chronic loneliness than even the loss of a loved one, and this is for several reasons:

★ Both parents involved usually emerge from the crisis with feelings of guilt, failure and depression, all of which provide fuel for loneliness.

★ The parent to whom custody of the children is entrusted, in an understandable desire to secure or retain their affection, will be under strong temptation to denigrate the estranged partner to the children.

★ The divorce may result in the total rejection of one spouse by the children, or—in the unhappy situation where different children favour different parents—they too become divided among themselves.

★ If the divorced mother entertains male friends in the home, the children are likely to feel in the way and not wanted.

★ Divorce usually springs from and generates conflict, which leaves scars on every member of the family unit. These may take a long time to heal.

Factors producing loneliness as a result of divorce are many. Although the marriage partnership may have been less than ideal, at least it provided a semblance of companionship for both partners. At least the home was not empty. There was someone there with whom to share, even though it might be superficially, the joys and trials of daily life; some-one with whom to consult when decisions must be made; someone to converse with at mealtimes.

The absence of these contacts creates an even more unsatisfactory situation. But too often this discovery is made only after the fatal step is taken. Then, too, the signing of the decree does not always take away the desire for physical intimacy. A com-fortable adjustment to the changed lifestyle is not achieved overnight. Coming home to a cold and empty house is no experience to be coveted.

UNWELCOME SIDE-EFFECTS
One of the unexpected and unwelcome results of divorce is that not infrequently friends begin to drop off, more especially if they are friends of the estranged spouse. They feel that they have to take sides. Invitations to social occasions come less fre-quently, because in our couples-orientated society a divorcee is sometimes regarded as a sexual threat.

An even more painful possibility may surface— the alienation of members of one's own family, with a consequent loss of love and support at the time when it is most needed.

The tragic factor is that a relationship which began with such high expectations, and in an atmosphere of love, has died. And now there is the legal process with all it involves—the division of assets and other necessary but heart-breaking deci-sions. It has been likened to an amputation. 'The pain is not over when the legal process has been finalised.'

A sense of failure in not having been able to make the marriage work, or in successfully fulfilling the role of a parent, does nothing to ameliorate the hurt or assuage the loneliness.

To the Christian, one of the most painful aspects of divorce emerges when, to their dismay, divorcees find that sometimes even fellow church members, friends of long standing, are cool and embarrassed in their relations. They do not know how to handle the situation. The fact that they may have made false assumptions concerning the facts of the case does not lessen the pain. The plain fact is that divorce always opens the door to possible misunderstanding, and even to unloving attitudes.

It must be emphasised, and strongly, that one essential element in alleviating the loneliness consequent on divorce is a genuine *forgiving from the heart* of the estranged partner, no matter how grievously he or she may have been at fault. An unforgiving spirit acts as a cancer in the soul.

Our Lord left no doubt as to the necessity of forgiving those whom we feel have sinned against us.

'When you stand praying, if you hold anything against anyone, *forgive him,* so that your Father in heaven may forgive you your sins.' (Mk 1.25: *italics mine*).

'Forgive us our debts, *as we also have forgiven* our debtors . . .' (Mt 6.12: *italics mine*).

10

THE LONELY UNEMPLOYED

The relentless onward march of electronics, automation, nuclear technology and computers, is leaving in its wake an ever-increasing company of the unemployed. A whole generation of young men and women, with all their unrealised potential, faces the grim prospect of going through life without ever obtaining a job.

An older generation, still willing and capable of doing valuable work, find themselves put out to grass, redundant. And the tragedy of their situation is that the prognosis for their ever gaining employment is bleak indeed. The physical and psychological effects of this situation are a matter of deep concern. The loneliness of the unemployed is one of the distressing maladies of our era for which no panacea has yet been found by politicians or business tycoons.

Until unemployment enters the arena of our own circle or personal experience, we are inclined to regard it as something regrettable but inevitable—a remote and unpleasant accompaniment of the march of progress. But when it invades our own circle and strikes us or our loved ones, the reality can be devastating.

Michael Holmes, a New Zealand journalist and public consultant, gave an interview which was published in a local newspaper, in which he frankly opened his heart and spoke for many of his fellow-sufferers. It was his desire to help those in a similar plight. I quote it at length, so that readers may gain a more realistic and compassionate view of what victims of this world-wide social ill have to contend with, and of the corrosive loneliness that results.

He talks freely of the manner in which unemployment affected him and his family. His case will be fairly typical of a large segment of unemployed people, except that he had the inner resource which comes through being a practising Christian. This proved to be the determining factor in his being able to survive the testing times.

He had attained a fairly comfortable position in life, and the possibility of becoming unemployed had never entered his thoughts. Thus it was something akin to an earthquake when he first became unemployed. The trauma continued for a total of 14 months, as he went through three prolonged periods of unemployment. He tells his story:

'I had always been a confident, self-assured person, but suddenly all that was stripped away and the reality and horror of unemployment had me in its grip. It seemed that I had missed the bus and was now a victim of society's work scrapheap. I felt devastated and thought the world had left me behind.

'True, I had made some errors of judgment,

but I never thought I would drop to such a low level of despair. My self-esteem crashed, and I felt worthless to myself, my family, my friends, the church, and even God Himself.

'The impression of rejection only consolidated as my position became clear, and hopelessness settled on me. I did not want to face people and found myself withdrawing into myself. I began to lose my self-confidence, and as the opportunity for work diminished with each job application, I found myself panicking as to whether I would ever get a meaningful job again.

'Bills still had to be met, teenage mouths fed, and the family still had to be motivated. Boredom is an emotional and spiritual killer, and time lay heavily on my hands as I waited anxiously for some response to many applications.

'The stigma of being unemployed is very real. To the employed and unemployed alike, unemployment is a social embarrassment. People are often nonplussed as to how to react, and often withdraw. Government agencies tend to treat you as less than a real person, and even prospective employers look at you with a jaundiced eye.

'Initially the full impact of what had happened was not too bad,' he writes. 'There was an air of optimism that all would be well in a week or two. However, as the weeks rolled into months, the clouds began to get darker.

'As the situation went from bad to worse (I applied for more than 100 positions earlier this year before I obtained my present temporary one), I began to realise that as a Christian I could no longer look to man for my solutions, but only

God was my ultimate deep emotional and spiritual anchor.

'Job's comforters were two-a-penny. Barriers went up. Well-meaning people, ignorant of what it is like to be unemployed and without too much thought for finer feelings, said things which made us feel hurt and distrustful. Having people say, "We think you should try such and such," or, "We think you are not doing enough about getting work," was frustrating.

'In a sense you got the feeling they were self-appointed "guardians" of the social security system, watching how we used the dole and how we lived. Often I gained the impression I and my family were an object of curiosity.

'Applying for a job when you are in your forties is almost an impossible task. I tried for all types of jobs, from Post Office commissionaire to chauffeur, and to more exotic positions. One of the biggest frustrations was applying for a job which wanted a mature and experienced person, only to find they wanted someone not over 25!

'Unemployment is a draining time, emotionally, physically and spiritually. But through it all we found our local church most supportive, and encouraging and practical. Well, you may ask, "Where is God through all this?" Like the psalmist I often asked myself why I was cast down, and always His answer came back, "Hope thou in God." My faith, background, life's experiences and Bible training and my church ministry enabled the Holy Spirit to bring many things to my remembrance.

'Patience is another ingredient. Even though I

was desperate, I am glad that God stopped me from getting certain jobs, proving the truth of Galatians 4.4—"in the fulness of time, God . . ." I have learned also that when you are in a position of comfort and affluence, it is so easy to speak glibly about trusting God.

'When you are down in the depths of despair, when faith is being put to the test, to be able to say, "I know whom I have believed and am persuaded that he is able to keep that which I have committed . . ." is a far more lasting and real truth.

'That's what God is all about. He is real when you are down. I have been there and know that God is able to do exceeding abundantly above all that I or my family could ever ask or think.

'As one of the unemployed, may I suggest that what we look for in our crisis is a spirit of discernment from those who come in touch with us. We don't want sympathy. Unemployment is a very personal and private thing. Don't try to understand it, or stand in judgment . . . After all, unemployment is a traumatic and a tender time for those who are its victims.'

This starkly honest account of the agonising experience many of our contemporaries are passing through, while bypassing none of the desolation of the experience, shows how the Christian, through his faith in God and the support of fellow-Christians, was enabled to triumph in the midst of tragedy.

11

THE LONELINESS OF LEADERSHIP

'On without cheer of brother or of
daughter,
Yes, without stay of father or of son,
Lone on the land, and homeless on
the water,
Pass I in patience till my work be
done.'

In his matchless poem, *St Paul,* F.W.H. Myers
puts these luminous words into the mouth of the
apostle. They certainly speak eloquently to his own
situation as he traversed land and sea with the
Good News. It was A.W. Tozer who said that most
of the world's great souls have been lonely. That
seems to be part of the price a saint must pay for his
saintliness. And it would be equally true that it is
usually part of the price of responsible leadership.

When Paul was immured in a Roman prison
awaiting his impending martyrdom, it was a very
human touch that he should beg his son in the faith,
Timothy, to come to him before winter, because he
was so lonely. Being a saint and a leader had not

lifted him above the need of congenial human companionship.

No one who has shouldered the burden of responsible leadership will find difficulty in identifying with Moses when he complained to God:

> 'I cannot carry all these people by myself; the burden is too heavy for me' (Num 11.14).

In every leadership position, crises will arise sooner or later, when the burden of responsibility seems far beyond one's ability to bear it. Paul found himself in such a position when ministering in the province of Asia.

> *We were under great pressure, far beyond our ability to endure,* so that we despaired even of life. Indeed in our hearts we felt the sentence of death. But this happened that we might not rely on ourselves, but on God who raises the dead' (2 Cor 1.8, 9: *italics mine*).

But the God in whom he trusted carried him through.

From its very nature the role of a leader must be a rather lonely one, for he must always be ahead of his followers in some areas. Though he or she be the most friendly and gregarious of people, inevitably there will be some paths they must be prepared to tread alone. It was Nietzsche's contention that life always gets harder near the summit—the cold increases and the path becomes more difficult. Mountain climbers affirm the truth that 'the higher you go, the lonelier it gets.'

This fact dawned dramatically on Dixon E. Hoste, one of the famous missionary 'Cambridge Seven' (which included Charles T. Studd), when J. Hudson Taylor, the founder of the China Inland Mission, passed the reins of leadership into the hands of his younger colleague. The China Inland Mission was the first of the so-called 'Faith Missions,' and was at that time the largest.

After the momentous interview during which the frail leader passed on the torch to his successor, Hoste, deeply moved and sensible of the weight of responsibility that now rested on his shoulders, said to himself: *'And now I have no one but God.'* Alone, yet not alone.

THE PRICE OF LEADERSHIP

Human nature craves companionship and it is a natural desire for a leader to wish to share with another or others the burden of his care, especially when decisions of far-reaching consequence must be made. It is heart-breaking at times for a leader to have to make adverse decisions affecting the future of loved colleagues—and make them alone. This is one of the costliest aspects of leadership, but sometimes it must be paid if one's leadership is to be productive.

Moses paid a steep price for his leadership— alone on the mount, and then alone on the plain. When his father-in-law, Jethro, came to pay his daughter and grandchildren a visit, he was appalled at the nervous and spiritual expenditure Moses's leadership was exacting. He tendered very sound advice, which Moses was wise enough to accept—advice which is equally apposite for today's over-burdened Christian leaders and executives who find themselves thrust into stressful situations.

> 'What you are doing is not good,' Jethro chided. 'You and these people who come to you will only wear your-selves out. The work is too heavy for you. You cannot handle it alone . . . Select capable men from all the people . . . and appoint them as officials . . . Have them serve as judges for the people at all times, but have them bring every difficult case to you' (Ex 18.17–22).

Moses found the answer to the isolation and loneliness of his leadership in the wise delegation and sharing of responsibility. His loneliness was more than the situation demanded, and only served to unfit him for his work. Those in leadership posi-tions are often slow to master this important lesson and pay the price in impaired health.

LONELINESS OF MISJUDGMENT
Moses experienced another painful type of loneli-ness—the crushing load of unjustified or jealous cri-ticism and misunderstanding.

> 'Miriam and Aaron began to speak against Moses because of his Cushite wife, for he had married a Cushite.

"Has the Lord spoken only through
Moses?" they asked. "Hasn't he also
spoken through us?" ' (Num 12.1, 2).

Though totally unselfish and disinterested in his
service for the nation, his motivation was impugned.
The fact that some of the criticism came from his
own sister and brother rendered it the more hurtful.

Tom Bracken evinced keen insight into the
nature of this kind of trial when he wrote:

> 'Not understood! We move along
> asunder;
>   Our paths grow wider as the seasons
> creep
> Along the years; we marvel and we
> wonder
>   Why life is life, and then we fall
> asleep,
>   Not understood.
>
> Not understood! How many breasts
> are aching
>   For lack of sympathy. Ah, day by
> day
> How many cheerless, lonely hearts are
> breaking,
>   How many noble spirits pass away
>   Not understood.
>
> O God! That men would see a little
> clearer,
>   Or judge less harshly when they
> cannot see!

*O God! That men would draw a littler
nearer
    To one another—they'd be nearer
Thee—
        And understood.'*

THE LONELY PROPHET

The prophets of Israel were lonely men. In the dawn of history the prophet Enoch walked alone in a decadent society, because his consistent walk with God necessarily led him in the opposite direction to that travelled by his ungodly contemporaries (Jude 14, 15).

Who experienced the pangs of loneliness more deeply than the prophet Jonah, as he trod the lonely streets of pagan Nineveh? It was to a city of a million inhabitants that he announced the unwelcome message of impending judgment: 'Forty more days and Nineveh will be overthrown' (3.4).

John the Baptist, the last and probably the loneliest of the long line of prophets, lived a great deal of his life in the solitude of the desert. His austere lifestyle and uncompromising message condemned him to a solitary life. And yet it was he who received from the Master a eulogy accorded to no other:

> 'I tell you the truth: Among those
> born of women there has not arisen
> anyone greater than John the Baptist'
> (Mt 11.11).

John did not permit his loneliness to deter him from exercising a mighty ministry. Has this something to say to the reader?

Today the loneliest preacher is probably the one to whom God has entrusted a prophetic message that cuts right across the prevailing temper of the age. The preacher who is ahead of his times is doomed to plough a lonely furrow.

The gregarious Paul often experienced the pangs of loneliness and bitterness of being misjudged and misunderstood by his contemporaries. More bitter still, even by some of his own children in the faith. Few things are more hurtful to a leader than the defection or desertion of friends or converts. What pathos Paul packs into these words:

> 'You know that everyone in the pro-
> vince of Asia has deserted me'
> (2 Tim 1.15).

Unfortunately, in our own day similar situations occur all too frequently.

In his book *The Team Concept*, Bruce Stabbert evaluates the advantage of a team ministry over against the one-man ministry with its inbuilt loneliness. He writes:

> 'There is an isolation and loneli-
> ness to the one-pastor ministry
> that is largely unnecessary. With
> a team there is a sharing of
> burdens in brotherly comity.

> 'Many pastors say that the ministry is
> lonely, but unavoidably so. Frequently
> a single pastor has no one in whom he
> can confide his frustrations, struggles
> and disappointments, with the excep-

tion of his wife. He may have no one to stand alongside him when he is too readily admonished by self-appointed critics.'[1]

The words of the wise man are singularly apposite in such a situation:

'Two are better than one, because they have a good return for their work. If one falls down, his friend can pick him up. But pity the man who falls and has no one to help him up! Also, if two lie down together, they will keep warm. But how can one keep warm alone?' (Ecc 4.9–11).

12

THREE CONTRIBUTORY ELEMENTS

LONELINESS OF TEMPERAMENT

The temperament with which one is endowed without doubt plays a significant part in determining the degree of one's vulnerability to the inroads of loneliness. Those blessed with a sanguine temperament with its optimistic window on life in general, should be less liable to fall prey to it than those whose temperament tends towards the melancholic.

In the melancholic person, feeling is a much more potent factor than it is with the sanguine. The former tends to be more introspective and withdrawn. He spends a good deal of time photographing his emotional states and developing the films.

This chronic inward-looking and often negative self-appraisal makes him self-absorbed, and thus a prime target for loneliness. However, that condition is not confined to the melancholic, for it can be experienced in differing degrees by every major personality type, given the conducive circumstances.

Of course none of us is responsible for the temperaments we have inherited, whether it be sanguine, melancholic or some other combination of types. But we are responsible for the way in which we react and control it. We are not caught helplessly in the grip of necessity, and need not remain its slaves. But unless we are alert and watchful of its tendency, we could easily become the plaything of our temperament. On the other hand we must guard against *the danger of regarding as spiritual failure what may be only an involuntary temperamental reaction in which there is no guilt.*

In treating this aspect of the problem, Dr Arthur T. Pierson suggested that we should be careful to 'distinguish between what is temperamental and what is properly spiritual in our human experience. In dealing with people, the sagacious counsellor will always draw a clear line of discrimination between what is impulsive and involuntary and what is deliberate and voluntary. Only the latter rightly belongs to the deeper spiritual life.

> 'There are traits inherited from immediate or remote ancestors that are no more a matter of personal choice than the colour of our hair or eyes, and therefore are destitute of proper moral quality.'[1]

We are not responsible for the capricious and involuntary undulations of our emotions—only for the definite choices of our will. We are what we choose, not what we feel. If we grasp this distinction, it could deliver us from the pain of much false guilt.

In referring to the inbuilt tendency of the melancholic to indulge in morbid, as opposed to constructive, introspection, Professor O. Hallesby of Norway had this to say: 'His introspection, however, may lead him to religious brooding. He has a tendency to devote himself to the more difficult passages of Scripture. These can turn him away from the Bible's simple statements about sin and grace, and thus weaken his spiritual life.'[2]

This adds up to the fact that the person of a predominantly melancholic turn of mind is more vulnerable to the experience of loneliness than any of the other temperaments—apart from the activity of grace, that is. But though he may give the impression of being distant and withdrawn, behind the sometimes forbidding exterior there beats a warm heart. The likelihood is that, though it may not be apparent, he has a secret longing for close companionship but does not know how to go about it.

At the other extreme are those who, in their desperate attempts to assuage their loneliness, may make such excessive demands on the time and affections of others that they actually defeat their own desire. Being over-possessive, or jealous and exclusive in a friendship, should be sedulously avoided if there is to be an easy and mutually enjoyable relationship.

THE DOUBTING MELANCHOLIC
Loneliness begets a negative frame of mind in which it is easier to see the darker side of life than the bright. The optimist sees the bottle half-full. The pessimist sees the same bottle half-empty. The same attitude persists in the depressed and lonely person's approach to Scripture. He finds it much easier to identify with the condemning passages

than with those that breathe assurance and confidence. But if we come to Scripture in that frame of mind, we will be likely to find what we expect.

A young woman who had doubts as to the factuality of Christ's bodily resurrection was asked to lead a study group at an Easter camp, and she was naturally in a quandary. How could she teach what she had doubts about herself? She consulted Miss Ruth Paxson, a well-known Bible teacher, and asked her to go through the resurrection passage in Matthew 28 with her. They came to verse 17: 'When they saw Him they worshipped him; *but some doubted*' (italics mine).

'How could they help doubting?' the girl said.

'Now isn't that strange,' replied Miss Paxson. 'When I read that verse, my thought was, 'How could they help worshipping?'

THE LONELINESS OF REJECTION

One common factor that contributes to loneliness is the experience of rejection, or the fear of being rejected. It is a condition most of us face sooner or later in some areas of life.

Once a person's friendly advances have met with coldness or rebuff, and especially so if he or she is shy and sensitive, it becomes increasingly difficult to summon up the courage to risk another rejection. Instead, the tendency will be to retreat further into oneself in order to avoid being hurt again.

Members of other ethnic groups who emigrate to our western lands all too often meet with a cool reception. Instead of receiving a warm welcome to their adopted homeland, they are ignored or rejected. In many cases they had escaped from their own disturbed country with high hopes of a new and better life opening out before them; but those hopes had been realised only partially and they have found themselves not fully accepted, lonely in a strange land. Immigrant workers who for periods leave their impoverished homelands to earn a precarious living in order to help support relatives they have left behind, meet with a very cold reception. Of course there are glorious exceptions, but the attitude outlined is far too common.

The indifference or at times exploitation which these newcomers experience in the host country, breeds a basic distrust of those who employ them or with whom they work. Having been rebuffed or ignored so often, they become hesitant to make further advances and retreat into their lonely ghettos.

A somewhat kindred attitude develops in some ageing people who feel—by no means always with just cause—that they are no longer needed or wanted by anyone. 'Of what use am I to anyone?' they moan. 'I am only a cumberer of the ground,' is the agonised cry of some neglected and rejected souls.

If they meet with further rejection, their understandable reaction is to doubt their self-worth yet more. Feeling that they are merely tolerated, not welcomed, they shrink back into their own sad little world.

Paradoxically, it is among the younger generation that loneliness is most prevalent and its pain most acute. The fear of lack of acceptance among their peers, or even outright rejection, in many cases becomes almost pathological. Even though it may be masked by boisterous or outrageous behaviour, the loneliness generated is intense, and we older people should be sensitive to this possibility and be reasonably tolerant in our attitude to them.

In her youth Margaret Mead, the noted anthropologist, went to De Pauw University filled with hope and excitement. She wanted to enter into campus life to the full, and in her mind this included the social life of a sorority. But her application for membership was declined. The wounds of that rejection cut deeply into the very core of her being. She survived the loss, but its effect was so great that later it made her very sensitive to the needs of excluded people. Doubtless that traumatic experience contributed greatly to her understanding of people of all races.[3]

But not every freshman is sufficiently resilient to emerge unscarred from so painful an experience as that suffered by Margaret Mead. In some, rejection causes great and permanent psychological damage which handicaps them for life. This in turn causes them to reject the friendly advances of others.

From the very nature of the case, as we have seen, divorce usually involves a mutual rejection of each other by the parties. In most cases it involves also the rejection of one parent or the other by the children. Loneliness is the inevitable fruit of the tragic event, and fuelled by the sense of guilt that has been engendered it can have profound effects on all parties involved.

Unfortunately, this state of mind can be further exacerbated by the rejection of family or friends. Had the parties been sufficiently wise and far-seeing to envisage the intensity of the loneliness their action would create and the wide sweep of the resulting consequences, there is little doubt many divorcees would have hesitated much longer before taking such a fateful and irrevocable step.

Experience attests that it is the person who takes the rejection or rebuff in his stride, rises and tries again, who will overcome the fundamental problem. The one who fails to do this and supinely succumbs, will in all probability lapse into even deeper isolation.

LONELINESS OF FAILURE

'Failure is one of the uglies of life,' wrote Howard Hendricks. And who of us can claim that we have not experienced failure? Whether Christian or non-Christian, we have all failed in some areas of our lives. There has been only One who has never failed.

With some, the failure has involved gross and disreputable sin. With others it may have been more respectable and socially acceptable sins, such as pride, envy, gossip and covetousness. But none will claim freedom from failure, except those who hold very superficial views of the sinfulness of sin.

An increasing number—Christian leaders and workers among them—are facing failure and breakdown in the marriage relationship, or in the area of parenting. Such failure was present in past days, but today it is much more difficult to conceal. It has grown alarmingly common and is open to public view. At the time of writing the failures of prominent Christian and political personalities are being flashed around the world, but evidence of regret and repentance on the part of some seems to be a missing element.

In many cases the failure is a lonely, personal secret, shared with no one else, but none the less distressing because of that. Loneliness is an inevitable concomitant of failure, because it is essentially personal. 'It was I who perpetrated it.' "I alone am responsible for it and the resulting consequences.'

Failure, the fear of exposure, and fear of further failure, readily lead the one who has failed to a withdrawal from intimacy with others, lest they discover what he or she is really like. The victims thus become the prisoners of their own thoughts and guilt. So, in order to preserve their reputation, they pursue the counter-productive course of retreating into themselves.

David followed this course, and as a result experienced the bitterness and loneliness of moral failure throughout the black year when he obdurately refused to repent and confess his sin with Bathsheba. Hear his tragic confession:

> 'When I kept silent, my bones wasted away through my groaning all the day long. For day and night your hand was heavy upon me; my strength was sapped as in the heat of summer. Then I acknowledged my sin to you, and did not cover up my iniquity. I said, "I will confess my transgressions to the Lord"—and you forgave the guilt of my sin' (Ps 32.3–5).

David's heart-broken sobs as he made confession of his sin in Psalm 51 are an indication of the sense of isolation from God which was the sure result of his unconfessed sin. The lesson for us is plain.

But note the shout of joy and release when, after his abject confession, he appropriated the divine forgiveness and burst out of the ice-house of his shame and loneliness:

> 'Blessed is he whose transgressions are forgiven and whose sins are covered. Blessed is the man whose sin the Lord does not count against him' (Ps 32.1, 2).

13

THE DEVIL'S PECULIAR WORKSHOP

'There are only two possible centres
for life—God and self. If we are not
becoming centred on God, we are
becoming centred upon self; and self-
centredness is the essence of sin. The
Jews—and we—may seek for the
Light of the World, the Light of life,
but so far as we remain self-centred,
we can never find it.'

Archbishop William Temple[1]

It was the Puritan saint William Law who described
self as 'the devil's peculiar workshop.' If he is
correct in his perception, then one of Satan's most
effective tools in achieving his subtle objectives
must be the scourge of loneliness.

'Indulging in self-pity is a one-way ticket to the
experience of loneliness,' says one counsellor; and
that is the voice of both commonsense and experience. The Christian who shifts the centre of life
from Christ to self thereby exposes himself to many
spiritual maladies. Because self-pity tacitly denies

personal responsibility for one's condition, there can be no successful strategy for conquering loneliness, so long as that attitude is indulged and maintained.

THE SNARE OF SELF-PITY

The classic biblical example of a true man of God who became engulfed in the morass of self-pity and loneliness is that of Elijah the prophet. It was after his epic encounter with Ahab and Jezebel, in which God gave him a notable victory, that his fall came.

The story is replete with instruction and encouragement for any who may be in like case. The root cause of his condition was diagnosed by God Himself, and He it was who prescribed the panacea. Elijah's sorry plight is epitomised in these words:

> 'Elijah was afraid and ran for his life.
> When he came to Beersheba in Judah,
> he left his servant there, while he him-
> self went a day's journey into the desert.
> He came to a broom tree and sat down
> under it, and prayed that he might die.
> "I have had enough, Lord," he said.
> "Take my life. I am no better than my
> ancestors."' (1Kg 19.3,4).

A more extreme example of depression, self-pity and loneliness it would be difficult to conceive, and as it is so relevant to the subject of our study, a detailed consideration of its lessons is warranted.

The satanic shaft struck Elijah when it would least have been expected. Surely elation would have been a more appropriate response. Had he not inflicted a stunning defeat on King Ahab, and had he not won a spectacular victory over the pagan god Baal and his followers?

But there were hidden reasons for his depression and loneliness, as there doubtless are with ours. What was it that caused him to cry mistakenly in his acute loneliness, 'I am the only one left, and now they are trying to kill me too' (1 Kg 19.10)?

There was *a physiological cause*. One has only to reflect on the tremendous emotional and physical expenditure involved in his confrontation on Mount Carmel—one lone man against a whole nation sunk deep in idolatry; then the extermination of the royally patronised priests of the alien god; to realise the magnitude of the reaction he now experienced.

Add to this the intensity of his prolonged praying, the long run to Jezreel, and his abstinence from food. He was both physically and emotionally exhausted. He discovered that the laws of nature function entirely without respect of persons and regardless of the merits of the cause that sparks the exhaustion.

Elijah was *utterly alone* in the desert, for he had left his servant a day's journey away—alone with himself, wallowing in an orgy of self-pity. One would have thought that after the excitement and exhaustion of the previous day he would have re- velled in the hours of solitude. But no! Instead, he turned inwards, and became vocally sorry for him- self. 'I have had enough, Lord,' he moaned, 'take away my life.'

There was also *a psychological cause* for his con- dition. In his hour of extreme reaction he actually reproached God for not adequately rewarding him for the zeal he had displayed in His cause.

'I have been very zealous for the Lord God Almighty,' he boasted. In strange disillusionment he said, 'I am no better than my ancestors'—tacit admission that he had been cherishing a secret sense of spiritual superiority. But now the falsity of his assertion is laid bare, for there were seven thousand Israelites who had not bowed the knee to Baal. His self-esteem was dealt a shattering blow. It seemed that all his zealous service had gone for nothing, unrecognised. He felt utterly let down— alone and lonely. 'I only am left.'

Elijah's sense of prophetic calling, which hitherto had been so strong, had now evaporated and he deserted his nation in her hour of need. Had he not prayed and toiled for a mighty spiritual revival to sweep over the land? But to all appearances the stirring had been superficial and ephemeral. He was an utter failure. Death would be preferable to life.

A COMPASSIONATE GOD

But his God is gracious and compassionate. He did not take His overwrought servant at his word, nor did He even reproach him. 'He knows how we are formed, and remembers that we are dust' (Ps 103. 14). Instead he dispatched an angelic messenger with a meal cooked in heaven's kitchen. The angel awakened Elijah and bade him eat. After he had satisfied his hunger, kindly sleep overcame him. The operation was repeated a second time.

Strengthened and refreshed by food and sleep, Elijah travelled 40 days and nights, 'until he reached Horeb, the mount of God.' Then he went into a cave and spent the night. Only then did God confront him with his fundamental problem. But for him there was no message in the tornado that shattered the rocks, or in the earthquake or the accompanying fire. It was not until 'after the fire there came a gentle whisper,' that God's message penetrated his lonely heart (1 Kg 19.12).

Any who may find themselves nearing the same condition should note and take comfort from the divine method with the overwrought prophet. In modern theological jargon, Elijah was an ideal example of 'burn-out.' He displayed all the authentic marks of that distressing condition.

What was the divine panacea? Two nourishing meals and two long sleeps. Only then, in a time of solitude, when he was in a fit state to hear God's 'voice of gentle stillness,' was he able to face his basic spiritual problem. Renewal of his depleted physical and nervous resources paved the way to a return to spiritual renewal and usefulness.

The lesson is obvious. It was only when Elijah was prepared to renounce his self-pity that God's gentle voice became audible to him. God does not shout His messages. Only then did the dove of peace return to his heart. Loneliness fled in the face of his renewed consciousness of the presence of God with him.

To his astonishment, God told him that far from being alone in his zeal and loyalty to Him, as he had supposed in his self-pitying mood, there were seven thousand others who also had refused to bow the knee to Baal.

Then the Lord assured him that he had not been laid aside because of his temporary defection. For him there was still a significant ministry to fulfil.

IMPORTANT SPIRITUAL LESSONS

Several important spiritual lessons emerge, which have a direct bearing upon the evil of self-pity with its consequent sense of loneliness and should be mastered by those who are lonely or depressed.

★ The Christian cannot with impunity break the laws of health, even though it be in an endeavour to meet the pressing needs of God's service and man's need. The fact that we are Christians does not render us immune from the penalty of broken natural law.

★ Times of solitude in which we withdraw from the rush and bustle of daily life are necessary wherever possible. It is then we may experience physical and spiritual renewal. It is at our peril that we overspend our physical and nervous capital.

★ If we shift our centre from Christ to self, we lay ourselves open to attack from our adversary and expose ourselves to other spiritual maladies.

★ What in our darker moments we see as failure, may sometimes be more apparent than real. In any case, no failure need be final. The road to cleansing and forgiveness is always open (1 Jn 1.9).

★ It was when Elijah threw off his self-pity and once again turned his eyes toward his compassionate God, that deliverance came. A renewed sense of the divine presence banished his unwarranted sense of loneliness.

THE PERIL OF SELF-CENTREDNESS

Another subtle manifestation of the self-life—life that revolves around oneself—is self-centredness; becoming almost totally absorbed in one's own interests and concerns. It is a well-known fact that people who are perennially lonely tend to move in this direction, only to find that their loneliness increases in proportion to their self-absorption.

> 'Self is the only prison that can ever bind the soul;
> Christ is the only Angel that can the gates unroll.
>   And when He comes to set thee free,
>   Arise and follow fast!
> His way may lie through darkness,
> But it leads to life at last.'

In referring to the benefits of wholesome and positive introspection, Dr W.E. Sangster wrote:

> 'The first thing that strikes any man or woman who seriously conducts this kind of self-examination, is how pre-occupied we are with ourselves—not only, or chiefly, when we are engaged in self-examination, but at all times. In the natural man, everything seems to have an immediate self-reference. The instant reaction of normal nature to any event or piece of news, or future possibility is, "How will this affect me?" The average man is far more distressed by a trifling mishap to

himself, than by a major calamity in someone else's life. Self-preoccupation is so natural and common that it is accepted as normal; it is only when we make ourselves face it that the enormity and distortion of our selfishness really appears.'[2]

It has been plausibly argued that without the aid of self-centredness, loneliness would find it difficult to exist. If we persist in focusing our thoughts upon ourselves, especially at a time when someone dear to us has been taken from our side, such an attitude will only fuel the fires of our desolation.

If the scriptural model is followed, the Christian life cannot be consistently selfish and self-centred. Christianity is uniformly presented as outward going, caring and concerned. To be Christlike, we will care so much for others that we largely forget ourselves.

Doctors tell of an uncommon nervous disease known as chorea, which causes the patient to turn round and continue to spin slowly on one spot—a condition strikingly similar to the conduct of the self-centred person. But all that self-absorption achieves is to imprison the soul in its own misery. Wholesome, constructive introspection can serve a useful purpose, but morbid self-scrutiny is counterproductive.

J. Gregory Mantle writes that in the Palace of Wurtzung there is a room the walls of which are hung with mirrors. It is called the Hall of a Thousand Mirrors. You enter. A thousand hands are stretched out to meet you, a thousand smiles greet your smile, a thousand pairs of eyes will weep when you weep. But they are all *your* hands, *your* smile, *your* tears. What a picture of the self-centred person! Self all around, self-multiplied.[3]

> 'There is a man who often stands
> Between me and Thy glory.
> His name is Self, my carnal Self
> Stands 'twixt me and Thy glory.
> O, mortify him, mortify him,
> Put him down my Saviour!
>   Exalt Thyself alone!
> Lift high the standard of the Cross
> And 'neath its folds
>   Conceal the standard-bearer.'

If instead of turning our eyes inward in self-contemplation we turn them outwards to other lonely hearts, setting ourselves to relieve their distress, we will find that in the process we are breaking out of the constricting shell of our own loneliness.

A friend with whom the author was travelling in Asia was killed in a plane crash on his way home. His widow, who was in very delicate health, at first was shattered by the unexpected tragedy. However, when time had in some measure alleviated the acuteness of her loneliness, she began to turn her thoughts away from her own sorrow to that of others in like case. 'How could my tragic experience be used by God to help other widows?' she asked herself.

As she prayed, the thought came to her. 'You are only one of thousands of widows who are grieving as you are. When you hear of someone who has been widowed, why not write to them and share your own experience of the comfort the Lord can give in the hour of need?'

She acted on this divinely inspired suggestion, and before long a whole new area of ministry opened up to her. When she read in the newspaper of someone who had been widowed, perhaps in an accident, perhaps in similar circumstances, she struck up a correspondence. Many were influenced to turn to God in their sorrow and desolation as a result of her concern. She found that as an unexpected side-effect, her own loneliness was largely dissipated.

She could very easily have been self-absorbed in her own grief, loneliness and ill-health. Instead she found the exquisite joy of mediating the comfort of God.

Out of his own experience, C.S. Lewis depicts in graphic, almost terrible terms, the danger in becoming self centred:

> *'If you want to keep it intact, you must give your heart to no one, not even an animal. Wrap it around carefully with hobbies and little luxuries; avoid all entanglements; lock it up in the casket or coffin of your selfishness. But in that casket, safe, dark, motionless, airless—it will change. It will not be broken, it will become unbreakable, impenetrable, unredeemable. The alternative to tragedy, or at least the risk of tragedy, is damnation. The only place outside of heaven where*

*you can be perfectly safe from all the
changes and perturbations of love, is
hell.'[4]*

One common characteristic of victims of loneliness is a tendency to blame others for their suffering.
But the cause is much more likely to lie at their own
door—in their own attitudes, whether conscious or
unconcious.

Self-centredness is natural in a child, but in an
adult it is childish, a patent mark of immaturity.
Our potential for loneliness is greatly increased
when we are preoccupied with ourselves, or when
we are unduly critical and intolerant of others. In
that state of mind and heart we exude an atmosphere that discourages others from desiring to enter
into a close relationship with us.

Charles Durham gives a shrewd analysis of the
self-centred life:

'The six undesirable personality traits
listed here, each have roots somewhere in self-centredness. The
reformers were often power-hungry,
the excessive talker needs to be at
centre stage, the competitor must be
the best, and the angry person must
have a vendetta. Boasting is often the
expression of excessive pride, or a
cover for personal insecurity.'[5]

To remedy this unhappy situation, we should
undertake a ruthlessly honest re-evaluation of our
attitudes, painful though the process may prove to

be. It will be well worth the pain. Then, having faced reality, heed Paul's injunction and 'Reckon yourself dead indeed unto sin—and self—but alive unto God.'

14

MINISTERING TO THE LONELY

In his *Rime of the Ancient Mariner*, Samuel Tayor Coleridge voiced the plaint of the lonely soul for whom no one seemed to care:

> *'Alone, alone, all all alone*
> *Alone on a wide, wide sea;*
> *And never a saint took pity on*
> *My soul in agony.'*

Ministering to the lonely people who surround us is never an easy task, even when we have the highest motivation and the utmost goodwill. Friendly advances are not always easy to make to a person in the grip of loneliness, nor are they always well received. Sometimes one will meet with a rebuff. A positive response on a first approach is unusual. Even though the sufferer may be aching for friendship, paradoxically for one reason or another he or she is loth to respond. It is for those who are concerned, and who do not labour under such a handicap, to be on the look-out for such persons, make the first approach and be prepared to accept an initial rebuff. In this way we can often break through the ice and open the way for further contact.

On one occasion when my wife and I had gone to the mountains for a time of retreat, she was brought to face anew the believer's responsibility for personal witness. Being of a shy and retiring disposition, she found witnessing to others a rather daunting experience. However, after meeting with the Lord at this time, she promised Him that henceforth she would be willing to witness for Him to any one, any time, anywhere. For her this was a costly commitment.

Only a day or two after our return to the city, as she was walking past an open-air evangelistic service, she noticed a young woman standing alone, listening to the message. As she passed her she felt the prompting of the Holy Spirit to go back and witness to her. Her recent resolve came to mind, so she retraced her steps.

On approaching the young woman, she discovered that she had only that day come to the city from the country, looking for employment. She knew no one and was desperately lonely. After further conversation she committed her life to the Lord, and later became a sincere Christian worker.

We who are enjoying the companionship of Christ should be sensitively alert to such opportunities, for we are surrounded by similarly lonely people who might be led to the Lord through a friendly touch, and find in Him the solution to their problem.

Lonely people often assume a protective mask to conceal their distress. We should be alert to pierce the mask and endeavour to overleap the barrier it creates.

In his *Macbeth*, Shakespeare very graphically poses a question that is relevant for the Christian worker:

> '*Canst thou not minister to a mind
> diseas'd,
> Pluck from the memory a rooted
> sorrow,
> Raze out the hidden troubles of the
> brain,
> And with some sweet oblivious
> antidote
> Cleanse the stuff'd bosom of that
> perilous stuff,
>   Which weighs upon the heart?*'

In ministering to the lonely, one productive avenue that can be followed is that of friendly hospitality. Shyness and reticence can more easily be overcome at the meal-table than anywhere else. Attractive food and a friendly exchange of conversation will help to loosen the tongue and create an atmosphere in which it will be easier for the sufferer to unbutton, and unburden himself or herself.

Those who have themselves trodden the same lonely path will be especially alive to the situation, and from the background of their own painful experience will be best equipped to help the fellow-sufferer out of his distress. The fact that we ourselves have known the comfort of God in our lonesomeness, lays on us the responsibility of mediating that comfort to others, as Paul says in 2 Corinthians 1. 3, 4:

'Praise be to the God and Father of our Lord Jesus Christ, the Father of compassion and the God of all comfort, *who comforts us in all our troubles, so that we can comfort those in any trouble* with the comfort we ourselves have received from God' (*italics mine*).

Kathleen Parsa recounts how simple assurance to a lonely woman that God really loved her brought relief from her loneliness.

'While travelling recently,' she writes, 'I encountered a lonely woman in her mid-twenties in a public rest-room. She was depressed and crying because she was far from her homeland of Ireland. She had also been drinking but seemed alert. After blurting out her story, she apologised.

'"I am sorry about this," she said.

'"Really, it's all right," I assured her. "I've been homesick before myself."

'"I had a couple of drinks, but instead of feeling happy, I feel so miserably alone," she confessed.

'"Are you a Christian?" I asked, feeling somehow that she might be.

'"Yes," she replied.

'"Then you know Jesus loves you?" I said.

'"She paused, looking me straight in the eye. "Yes," she said slowly, "He does."

'"Well, even though you *feel* alone, you are *not* alone, ever. He's always with you and He'll always love you." I gave her a quick hug and said, "I'll be praying for you."

'With that I hurried out, but not without first

noticing a change in her countenance. She was smiling, and seemed calmer.'[1]

For those who desire to help the lonely, opportunities abound on every hand. Visitation in homes for the elderly is much appreciated by those who seldom have a visitor. Many old people who live alone in their own homes would eagerly welcome a visitor and enjoy a friendly chat.

For those who are in frail health, an offer to cut the lawn, or do other odd jobs which they are unable to do for themselves, would be a godsend. In such an atmosphere of goodwill it is not difficult to bring a message of comfort or salvation from the Scriptures.

But it must be borne in mind that ministry to the lonely can be a costly, time-consuming and at times disappointing experience. We cannot genuinely help others without 'virtue' going out of us—physical and nervous force. To be effective in this area of service will involve us in so identifying ourselves with our friends as to enter into their experience as though it were our own.

PART II

PRESCRIBING THE CURE

15

ON THE ROAD TO RELIEF

It is much easier to diagnose the nature of physical malady than to prescribe the appropriate remedy—and it is no different with maladies of the spirit, of which loneliness is one. They are so diverse in origin, so varied in incidence and so different in manifestation.

In the doctor-patient relationship, the most satisfactory results are secured when there is complete openness and sincerity on the part of both doctor and patient. So must it be if the cause of the loneliness is to be correctly diagnosed and the longed for remedy prescribed and acted on. And as with medicine, the most helpful draught is often the most unpleasant to take. It is only the immature person, however, who refuses to swallow the curative medicine because it tastes unpleasant!

Without hesitation I would lay it down as axiomatic that if loneliness is to be overcome, *it must be accepted that the initiative in relieving the condition lies with the sufferer himself or herself. It is they who must take the first step,* and set the machinery for recovery in motion. If they are unwilling to do this, they are likely to be left with their loneliness.

Ultimately we must face reality and take responsibility for our condition. It is our *personal* loneliness, and for it we have final responsibility. So if any change is to be effected, it is we who must take the initiative. If we choose to deny responsibility and blame others for it, the prospect for release is dim. We must cease blaming parents, environment, or other people or circumstances, or there can be no effective strategy for conquering the malady. There is good hope for release when we accept that, in the end, we and no one else are responsible to create the conditions for change.

CLEARING THE GROUND

Loneliness is by no means always spiritual in origin, but spiritual factors may very well be accentuating the problem. Since this is very likely to be the case, the ground of our lives should be cleared of all noxious elements, so that the Holy Spirit can work unhindered in the soil of our hearts. If there are things we know to be wrong, or about which the Holy Spirit has been convicting us, these should be honestly confessed with no excuses or secret reservations. One evidence that our confession is sincere will be that our sins are not only confessed, but renounced.

> *'Repentance is to leave the sins*
> *We loved before,*
> *And show that we in earnest grieve,*
> *By doing them no more.'*

If a secret resentment against the Lord is cherished

in the heart—and this is often the case, though not openly expressed—this attitude must be corrected. God purposes only good for His child. 'He disciplines us *for our good,* that we may share His holiness' (Heb 12.10: italics mine). We must be right with God before we can be right with ourselves and others.

This process may be likened to the lancing of a suppurating sore. Before the healing process can begin, the offensive material must be drained off.

When we come to Him in true penitence, God is very gracious. We need entertain no fear of rebuff or rejection, no matter how unworthy we feel and are. His attitude to His failing children is beautifully exhibited in the revelation of Himself God gave to Moses when he prayed, 'I beseech you, show me your glory' (Ex 33.11).

> 'The Lord came down and proclaimed his name, The Lord, the Lord, the compassionate and gracious God, slow to anger, abounding in love and faithfulness, maintaining love to thousands, and forgiving iniquity, rebellion and sin' (Ex 34.6, 7).

APPROPRIATING FORGIVENESS
A gift does not become ours until we appropriate it. God freely offers forgiveness for all our sin, and acceptance of that forgiveness is another important milestone on the road to restoration. Lonely people usually tend to be self-condemnatory. They see in their condition some real or imaginary fault of their own, for which they find it hard to forgive themselves.

But if our holy God is willing, for Christ's sake, to forgive us on confession, then surely we can forgive ourselves for the sins He has forgiven. Hear His assuring words:

> 'Their sins and their iniquities I will remember no more for ever.' (Heb 8.12).

Why should we keep on remembering and tormenting ourselves, when God assures us He has not only forgiven our sins, but forgotten them as well? Is that not culpable unbelief that grieves His loving heart?

One writer termed forgiveness, 'this amazing therapeutic agent.' He asserted that to be able to forgive affords such a relief to the soul, that it is all the relief many need. So, if there is someone whom we have not forgiven for some injury suffered, that is a stumbling-block that must be removed.

So avail yourself of the therapeutic power of God's proffered forgiveness. Take Paul's inspired advice and 'forget the things that are behind' (Phil 3.13). Resolutely slam and lock the door on past sin and failures, and throw away the key! Then strain forward to the better things that lie ahead.

Do not wait passively (and hopelessly) for someone else to do something about your loneliness. Look life in the face and step resolutely forward. Face reality, and adjust to it.

Recently, in counselling a young man who had retreated from life as the result of some very painful experiences, I discovered that through discouragement he had dropped out of social life and had become a 'loner.' I encouraged him to make a new beginning the very next day; to ask God to enable him once again to establish contact with his fellows and begin serving the Lord again.

The very next evening he came to me with beaming face. He had approached a non-Christian neighbour whom he found responsive to his advances. The neighbour had actually invited him to come and do some Bible study with him! God does not take long to answer the sincere prayer of one who desires to be right with Him.

SELF DISCLOSURE
Another helpful step in coping with loneliness is to *unburden oneself to God* uninhibitedly, just as the psalmist often did. Be open and honest with Him. Tell Him exactly how you feel. He is your heavenly Father, whose sympathetic ear is always open to His children's woes.

> 'He knows how we were formed
> He remembers that we are dust' (Ps 103.4).

> '*Pour out your heart* to him, for he is our refuge' (Ps 62.8: *italics mine*).

Further, if there is some mature Christian whom you feel you can trust, unburden yourself to him or her. A burden shared is often a burden halved. Share your feelings and failures, your struggles and fears—and your joy as well. In other words, 'unbutton' yourself, reveal yourself, weaknesses and all. You will be amazed at the sympathetic hearing you will receive, as well as the therapeutic value of such self-disclosure.

IN ACCEPTANCE LIES PEACE

'In acceptance lies peace' has become almost a spiritual cliché, but it enshrines an important spiritual and psychological truth. We cannot change our outward circumstances. These are beyond our control, and we are responsible only for things under our control. But we could, and should, change our inward attitude to them. *By present action we can modify the future.* Where no alternative seems possible, it is only commonsense to come to terms with life. While this is admittedly a difficult lesson to master, it is an essential one.

Two friends of the author had six children, three of whom were subnormal both physically and mentally. In the early stages of this experience, my friends found it desperately hard to accept this as being God's will for them; they struggled against it and questioned why this should have happened to them. But they found that, far from helping the situation, they were only hurting themselves and spoiling their lives.

Then, like Jacob, they had a transforming encounter with the Lord. Finally, they accepted the fact that God had permitted this trial and that 'in all things God works for the good of those who love him, who have been called according to his purpose' (Rom 8.28).

'Once we had accepted it as God's will for us,' the wife told me, 'we learned in experience the truth we had known in theory, that in acceptance lies peace, and we were able to triumph in the midst of the trial.' But she added this significant word:

'Once we had accepted it as the will of God, it couldn't hurt us any more.' So they emerged from the trial enriched, not impoverished.

Note that they *accepted* the will of God while still in the midst of the trying circumstances, difficult though they were. Then they *adapted* to the adverse circumstances; and those who knew them testified that they *adorned* the painful situation. Those three words—accept, adapt, adorn—carry their own message.

It can be so with our loneliness; we can accept it as God's will for us, and also accept the responsibility of triumphantly coping with it. If we react rightly, the whole experience can have a positive benefit. In accepting instead of resenting and rebelling, we will find ourselves better able to accept ourselves and others. In the final analysis, the determining factor in the battle with loneliness is our attitude to it.

The lonely person faces only two possible choices, and the choice he or she makes will determine the possibility of relief. He must either *rise above* the loneliness, or *succumb* to it and continue to suffer the consequences.

One can run away from life—and many are taking the suicide route—or look the facts in the face and meet them with the courage God will give.

Now we are in a position to consider some possible courses of action—some have already been mentioned—that may greatly ameliorate or even cure our malady.

16

PALLIATIVE, NOT PANACEA

When one is marooned in the arid wastes of loneliness, concerned and well-meaning friends—out of the kindness of their hearts—proffer advice and nostrums which they hope will be of help. But while the kindly gesture is appreciated, the suggestions usually do little to alleviate the anguish of heart. Suggestions like taking a travel holiday, joining an encounter group or buying new clothes, coming at a time when the suffering is acute, are as helpful as telling a neurotic person not to worry or a depressed person to cheer up. They seem to bear no relation to the realities of the situation.

Some such activities doubtless may prove helpful in affording temporary distraction and relief, but they are only a palliative, not a panacea, for they touch only the surface of the problem. Sooner or later reality must be honestly faced and the root cause searched out and dealt with.

Alfred Lord Tennyson wrote of the pallid consolations that were extended to him in the tragic hour when his dearest friend was snatched away to a premature grave:[1]

PALLIATIVE, NOT PANACEA

'One writes that "other friends remain,"
That loss is common to the human
race;
And common is the commonplace,
And vacant chaff, well-meant for
grain.

That loss is common does not make
My own loss less bitter, rather more;
Too common! Never morning wore
To evening, but some heart did break.'

The newly-bereaved widow, for example, is often encouraged by her friends to begin a new career and build a new life for herself. The advice is correct and sound and probably will be acted upon, *but at a later date*. Then it will have meaning for her. But none of these can fill the *present* aching void.

Travel, with its new scenes and varied interests, does afford some distraction, but the trouble is that, wherever we go, we take our loneliness with us; we cannot leave it at home. And when we return from our travel or other activity, we will find it awaiting us when we enter the familiar door. Travel is helpful, but it is only a palliative.

In the rupture of a treasured relationship or in the desolation of bereavement, it is inevitable that we feel acutely alone in our sorrow and loss. It is not that our friends have failed us, or do not love us deeply and desire to help, but they have each other, and their own interests claim their attention. They have other things to talk about and share, and may have troubles of their own. But we are shut up with our own lonely heart and there seems no end to the dark tunnel in which we find ourselves.

At first, the very prospect of taking life up again seems too painful to contemplate. Someone must keep the memory of the loved one alive. It would seem almost callous to allow life to go back to normal again, as though nothing has happened.

OUTWARD EXPRESSION OF GRIEF

In the shallowness of our modern lifestyle, the outward expression of grief tends to be suppressed, especially on the part of men. But that suppression serves only to generate a deeper loneliness. Grief should be freely expressed, by men as well as women.

In my youth there was a much greater open expression of sorrow and sympathy at the loss of a loved one. Relatives went into mourning, sometimes for as long as six months. Women wore black dresses. Men, and boys even, wore black arm-bands. Handkerchiefs and stationery were edged with black. This was done as a sincere and tangible expression of shared grief and respect.

A return to those practices is not being advocated, but they did allow sorrow and grief to have wholesome and overt expression. It indicated to the bereaved person that they and their loved one were not forgotten.

The prevailing tendency, however, is to avoid talking about the one who has died, for fear of embarrassing the relict. But the fact is that, in most cases, the grieving person wants to do that more than anything in the world. Talking about them keeps alive the treasured memory in a wholesome, not a morbid, manner. To be able to talk about a departed loved one in a natural way is a most valuable therapy.

The lonely heart, as we have seen, seeks escape from its prison house in many ways. Some flee from reality by plunging into a round of frenzied activity, in the vain hope that this will fill the endless hours and perhaps induce a period of forgetfulness. Others resort to excursions into the world of entertainment, but find that it provides only fleeting relief.

The murky world of the occult makes its appeal to those who desire to re-establish contact with loved ones beyond the veil. Eastern mystery religions have become very popular and are increasingly making their appeal to a segment of society, disillusioned and lost. But all alike prove a delusion and disappointment.

'Everyone has escapes,' writes Nancy Potts. 'Some people over-eat, others watch TV soap operas, become workaholics, enter on non-stop activities . . . try to dull the pain with alcohol or drugs. The possible ways to escape are endless. However, the end result is self-pity and a loss of self-respect.'[2]

This is not to say that some of these escapes do not in measure meet a need, but the relief they give is short-lived. They are not a panacea, only a palliative. A bandaid is useful to cover a cut, but is not of much help to a broken arm. Tranquillisers may afford temporary relief, but address only the periphery of the problem. They fail to treat the real focus of infection from which the loneliness stems.

The round of pleasure or the amassing of wealth are but vain attempts to escape from the persistent ache. It is a well-known fact that the millionaire is usually a lonely man, and the comedian is often more unhappy than members of the audience he is entertaining.

Even success does not always fill the aching void, as the brilliant Henry Martyn discovered. At the age of 20, as a student at Cambridge University, he gained the highest honours the world had to offer in mathematics. But when the celebrations were over, Martyn said that, instead of his success bringing fulfilment, 'to my surprise I found that I had only grasped a shadow.'

Later he went to India as a missionary. When he reached that land, he knelt on the shore and prayed, 'And now let me burn out for God.' He lived for only seven more years, but in that short time he gave the world translations of the New Testament in three difficult Eastern languages. Those three New Testaments were no shadow!

Byron the poet made the same discovery and wrote of it in these lines:

> 'Although gay companions o'er the bowl
> Dispel awhile the sense of ill,
> Though pleasures fill the maddening soul,
> The heart, the heart is empty still.'

NO SIMPLE CURE
The unadorned fact must be faced that one's loneliness will not be dissipated by any simple or single procedure. It is usually too deeply ingrained into one's personality and emotional make-up to respond to anything but radical treatment.

Nor will the final answer be found in forming a

number of casual relationships. It will be discovered in forming *quality* relationships with congenial persons. It is not the *number of friends* we gain that is important, but rather the *quality of relationship* we establish. As Seneca said, 'We are born to live together.' Life is not complete alone.

In each of us there is a deep psychological need and desire for a warm companionship that will survive the tests of time and modern pressured life. Even our divine Lord, self-sufficient though He was, in his human nature craved the friendship and support of His intimates. Under stress their friendship proved imperfect, but it was something He appreciated deeply. Indeed, He paid a lovely tribute to their loyalty in the memorable words: 'These are those who continued with me from the beginning' (Lk 22.28).

Intimacy with sympathetic and understanding friends *can* and *does* alleviate the pangs of loneliness. And although it may prove difficult to achieve that intimacy, *it is possible* if approached in the right manner and with purpose of heart.

17

THE BALM OF FRIENDSHIP

'Friendship is a thing most necessary
to life—since without friends, no one
would choose to live, though possessed
of all other advantages.'

Aristotle

A warm, stable friendship is one of the most precious gifts life has to offer. Its absence is one of life's greatest deprivations. Altogether apart from the mutual joy which they derive from the relationship, friends are one of the most effective barriers against loneliness.

In his useful book, *Friends and Friendship,* Jerry White defines friendship in these terms: 'A friend is a trusted confident to whom I am mutually drawn as a companion and ally, whose love for me is not dependent on my performance, and whose influence draws me nearer to the Lord.'[1]

In a true friendship there is a mutual willingness for each to accept the other *just as they are,* 'warts and all.' Those who establish such a relationship are rich indeed.

148

George Elliott charmingly describes the luxury of such a friendship; 'O the inexpressible comfort of feeling safe with someone, having to weigh neither thoughts nor measure words, but pour them all out just as they are, chaff and grain together; and a faithful hand will take and sift them, keep what is worth keeping, and with a breath of kindness, blow the rest away.'

When Jeremy Taylor, the old Puritan, had his house burgled, all his choicest possessions taken and his family turned out of doors, he knelt down and thanked God that his enemies had left him the sun and moon, a loving wife and *many friends to pity and relieve,* the providence of God, all the promises of the gospel, his faith, his hope of heaven, and his charity towards his enemies!

With wealth such as this, no burglar could impoverish him, for true riches do not consist merely in material things. 'Many friends to pity and relieve.'

THE RISK OF FRIENDSHIP

It is the 'how' of establishing a friendship that creates the problem for the lonely person. Either by choice or by exclusion they find themselves isolated from their fellows. As we have seen, either by shyness or the fear of possible rebuff, they have been held back from attempting friendly approaches.

They feel it almost impossible to take the first step towards closer contact with others. And yet, if there is to be any relief from loneliness, *those advances must be made, and made by them.* Otherwise they will continue to be confined in their self-constructed prison-house. It is a well-proved principle that 'a man that hath friends must shew himself friendly' (Prov 18.24 KJV).

> *'There are hermit souls that live with-*
> *drawn*
> *in the peace of their self-content.*
> *There are souls that dwell like stars*
> *apart*
> *in a fellow-less firmament.*
> *There are pioneer souls who blaze*
> *their paths*
> *where highways never ran,*
> *But let me live in a house by the side of*
> *the road*
> *and be a friend of man'*[2]

There are ways, however, by which even the shy and withdrawn person can overleap this barrier, but it will take a deliberate act of the will to locate and establish and maintain the friendship. 'We tend to believe that friendship depends on meeting the right people. God in His Word tells us it depends on our being the right person.'

One researcher circulated a questionnaire prob-ing the nature of friendship. In every answer he received, the respondent said that those closest to them were people willing to disclose their feelings and needs. 'We often fail to open ourselves to others from fear of rejection. If you open up, you take a risk, you become vulnerable.'[3]

That is undoubtedly true. But *is the alternative if we do not take the risk, more acceptable*? It means an unending perpetuation of the painful *status quo*.

Ralph Waldo Emerson asked a pertinent ques-tion: 'We take care of our health, we lay up money, we keep our roof tight and our clothing sufficient, but who provides wisely that he shall not be wanting in the best property of all—friends?'

True friendship can be costly. It is much more than making use of someone for our own benefit, for of necessity it involves self-giving, and that incurs a cost. It was said of a wealthy and generous man that with all his giving, he never gave himself. He thus withheld the most precious gift of all.

FRIENDSHIP CAN TRANSFORM

A young girl who had attended her first holiday camp, on returning home was asked whether she had felt lonely or homesick. Her ingenuous reply was, 'I had no time to be lonely, because I was so busy keeping other girls from being homesick that I never thought of being homesick myself.' What a window into the way out of loneliness! It is the self-occupied person who feels its sharpest pangs. Friendliness begets friendship and in the process banishes loneliness.

The establishing of a friendship at a critical juncture in the young Hudson Taylor's missionary career, played a significant part in the whole of his subsequent missionary achievements. After he had experienced two crushing blows, God brought into his life a godly Scottish minister, William C. Burns, a man about 20 years his senior. Burns had been the human instrument in a powerful spiritual revival at the church of the saintly Robert Murray McCheyne in Dundee.

For seven months the two friends worked and travelled and prayed together, months which left an indelible impression on the younger man. One of the biographies of Hudson Taylor highlights the importance of that timely friendship. It was rightly said that Burns saved Taylor from himself. Rejected by conventional missionaries as he was, he might have grown into an isolated prig, for he was far ahead of his times. He might have developed into an individualist moving in steadily contracting circles, leaving little behind but a few converts and an awkward memory. Instead, he became a trailblazer of the modern missionary movement.

He received from Burns an imprint that was never obliterated. His experience exemplified the value of a quality friendship which came at a time when, in his loneliness, he might have turned in on himself.

THE IMPORTANCE OF LOYALTY

Once a friendship has been established, it should be kept in mind that mutual loyalty is essential if it is to flourish and endure. One researcher discovered that the qualities most appreciated in a friendship were: the ability to keep a confidence; loyalty; warmth and affection; the ability to have intimate conversations. Those in search of friendship should bear these findings in mind, for it is a two-way business.

Confidences should be kept sacrosanct and not shared with others, even for prayer, *without the consent of the friend*. Many promising friendships have foundered because this factor has not been observed.

Dr Ben Johnson gave this counsel: 'A man should always keep his friendship in repair.' One way of doing this when separated is through a warm correspondence. This will build an added dimension to the relationship.

A friendship flourishes and deepens in proportion to what each party puts into it. It must be worked at and mutual unselfishness is a valuable component. Working together in social or Christian service will forge a close bond.

Paul the apostle possessed the ability to gain and retain the loyalty of his friends of both sexes and all ages, to a remarkable degree. The secret of this gift peeps out in all his letters—*his capacity for unselfish and undemanding love.* He was prepared to pour it out without stint, even if it met with no return.

> 'I will very gladly spend for you all I
> have, and expend myself as well. If I
> love you more, will you love me less?'
> (2 Cor 12.15).

F. W. H. Myers captures this quality in his poem, *St Paul.*

> *'Hearts I have won, of sister or of*
> *brother,*
> *Quick on earth, or buried in the sod,*
> *Lo, every heart awaiteth me, another*
> *Friend in the blameless family of God.'*

But there is a friendship that is even more important and wonderful, which should be cultivated sedulously. A friendship which, if truly embraced and responded to, will banish loneliness. The wise man of the Proverbs wrote:

'There are friends who pretend to be friends, but *there is a Friend who sticks closer than a brother*' (Prov 18.24 RSV: *italics mine*).

'*Many names are dear, but His is dearer,*
    How it grows more dear as life goes on;
Many friends are dear, but He is dearer,
    Always what we want, and all our own.
Jesus, Jesus, let us ever say it
    Softly to ourselves as some sweet spell;
Jesus, Jesus, troubled spirit lay it
    On thy heart, and it will make thee well.'

A.J. Foxwell

18

PSYCHOLOGICAL AND SOCIAL ELEMENTS

Some writers who approach this subject from the Christian point of view, focus mainly on spiritual solutions. These are undoubtedly relevant and of prime importance, but there are psychological factors involved which should not be ignored. The New Testament blends both approaches.

THE PSYCHOLOGICAL ELEMENT

Before considering what practical steps can be taken to resolve the problem, one's thinking must be clarified, for it is in the thought life that the battle for victory must be fought and won.

It must be accepted that *some degree of loneliness is a natural component of ordinary living*. No one escapes its inroads altogether. The fact that loneliness was an element in the experience of our sinless Lord when He assumed our human nature argues this. We are private beings who do not always admit even our dearest friends into all areas of our private lives.

There are certain walks of life, for example, in which some degree of loneliness is inevitable. Responsible top leadership necessarily involves it, for important and far-reaching final decisions have to be made alone—they cannot be shared.

Again, life is so complex that *we have to learn to live with some problems of body and mind.* God does not remove every adverse circumstance from the path of the Christian or provide easy explanations and solutions to every mysterious dealing. Life would be greatly impoverished were this not so. It is wrestling with adverse circumstances that builds moral and spiritual muscle. If life were all easy and uncomplicated, we would become little better than the spineless jelly-fish. While God may allow the thorn to remain, He will also give adequate grace to bear it (2 Cor 12.9).

In a moment of self-revelation, Malcolm Muggeridge paid striking testimony to the enduring value of the unexplained and painful experiences of life.

'Contrary to what might be expected, I look back on experiences that at the time seemed especially desolating and painful with particular satisfaction. Indeed, I can say with complete truthfulness that everything I have learned in my 75 years in this world, everything that has truly enhanced and enlightened my existence, has been through affliction and not through happiness, whether pursued or attained.

'In other words, if it were ever to be possible to eliminate affliction from our earthly existence by means of

some drug or medical mumbo-jumbo
. . . the result would not be to make
life delectable, but to make it too
banal and trivial to be endurable.'[1]

It is the tree which has to withstand the fiercest
storms that becomes deep-rooted and strong. The
fight to overcome or compensate for our loneliness
may well prove to be the very agent that drives us to
God and makes us strong in ourselves, and therefore able to help others in a like condition.

IMPORTANCE OF SELF-DISCLOSURE

If the healing process is to progress, there must be
some degree of self-disclosure to someone, a
willingness to open and expose oneself. The very
articulation of our emotions often sets us on the
road to release. If loneliness has caused bitterness,
resentment, envy or self-pity, open your heart first
to God and confess these sins, for all sin is primarily
against God (Psalm 51.4). Then, if there has been
sin against another person, confess it to him or her.
We have the healing assurance from God,

'If we confess our sins, he is faithful
and just and will forgive us our sins
and purify us from all unrighteous-
ess' (1 John 1.8).

Confession and acceptance of God's promised
forgiveness help to get these negative and harmful
attitudes out of our system, and will bring unimag-
inable release. If you can share your emotional
problem with another human being, that will also

have a most helpful therapeutic effect. *Friendship develops and deepens with mutual self-disclosure,* for it provides an outlet for the pent-up emotion that produces the loneliness.

It is instructive to note that in the lonely year during which King David was unwilling to open himself and confess his sin with Bathsheba, his attitude locked him into himself. But when he articulated it in sincere confession, his spirit broke free:

> 'When I kept silent, my bones wasted away through my groaning all the day long. For day and night your hand was heavy on me; my strength was sapped as in the heat of summer. *Then I acknowledged my sin to you and did not cover my iniquity.* I said, "I will confess my transgressions to the Lord"—*and you forgave* the guilt of my sin' (Ps 32.3–6: *italics mine*).

There is no one, however competent and confident they may appear, who does not have some areas of weakness and some negative attitudes to overcome. We are not unique in that respect. While we cannot change our circumstances, we can change our attitude towards them. Instead of allowing them to shape our lives, we can make them tributary to our growth in maturity. It is only common wisdom to accept what can't be changed and endeavour to change what can be changed.

One reason which might prevent self-disclosure could be a distrust of others. We may feel that if we reveal what we really are like, we will be rejected or betrayed. This is, of course, a possibility. But if we are ever to break free from our bondage, it is a risk that must be taken. Generally speaking, it will be found that our fear was without foundation. But when the alternative of continuing to live with our unrelieved loneliness is considered, it is a risk well worth taking. Retreating into one's shell achieves nothing.

AVOID SELF-DEPRECIATION

A habit which should be resisted is *the tendency to depreciate oneself.* This can be at the same time the cause and the result of loneliness. The person who has an unduly low level of self-esteem is especially vulnerable. While we must abjure pride and vanity, Scripture encourages us to make an honest self-appraisal, neither exalting ourselves on the one hand nor depreciating ourselves on the other. Paul emphasises this in Romans 12.3:

> 'As your spiritual teacher I give this piece of advice to each one of you. Don't cherish exaggerated ideas of your importance, *but try to have a sane estimate of your capabilities* by the light of the faith God has given to you all' (J.B. Phillips).

This does not mean that we are to be satisfied with ourselves as we are—we should be aiming higher, always—but we must not fly to the opposite extreme and devalue ourselves. We should guard against devaluing what God valued so highly as to consider it worth the sacrifice of His Son.

Paul is not speaking here of self-occupation but sane self-evaluation. While he confessed, 'I know that nothing good lives in me, that is, in my sinful nature' (Rom 7.18), that fact did not prevent his honest self-appraisal when he claimed, 'I do not think I am in the least inferior to these super-apostles' (2 Cor 11.5).

God's evaluation of us is more accurate than our own. He knows all about us, for He made us. His estimate of our worth in His sight is measured by the fact that He gave up His Son for us. He has no favourites, for 'with Him there is no respect of persons.' Others may seem more attractive and worthy in our eyes, but none is more precious to God than we are.

Paul mastered the secret of handling adverse circumstances.

> '*I have learned* to be content whatever the circumstances. I know what it is to be in need, and I know what it is to have plenty. *I have learned the secret* of being content in every situation . . . I can do everything *through him who gives me strength*' (Phil 4.11–13: *italics mine*).

To discover the kind of circumstances he learned to triumph over, read 2 Corinthians 11.23–28! But note that he emphasises that it had been a learning process. He had not always been content. He persevered and mastered the secret, through the strength he drew from Christ.

Since self-absorption proves counter-productive

in relieving loneliness, the most helpful and sensible alternative is to turn one's thoughts outward to others who may be even more lonely. Think of ways in which you might minister to their need. Think of lonely and neglected children, lonely widows and widowers, lonely divorcees, lonely immigrants or international students. Indeed, your next-door neighbour may be facing the very same problem, without your suspecting it.

In every heart there is the insatiable longing, not always recognised as such, to be loved and appreciated. *Form the decision to relate to some such person or persons, and then DO IT*.

THE SOCIAL ELEMENT

It is in the area of social relationships that the problem lies. The root of loneliness is the absence of loving and satisfying companionship, and it is here a change must be made.

It is taken for granted that the reader is sufficiently in earnest to find a remedy for his or her condition as to be willing to take positive steps towards a solution. Without this sincerity, no suggestion will be of much help. As we have seen, there are only two alternatives—*transcend or succumb*. The decision to take steps to relate to others is a simple decision of the will, difficult though it may be. But it can lead to a transformed life.

SUGGESTED STEPS

After prayer, think of the most likely person to whom you could make friendly overtures; then seek a favourable opportunity for your contact. Consider the most suitable approach you could make.

Practise the art of opening and continuing a conversation.

If there are common interests, begin with those. It will be found that one of the most productive methods is to get the other person talking about himself and his interests. This creates a relaxed atmosphere. Being an interested listener paves the way for further communication. Let your interest in him be genuine and you will soon find that you can forget yourself.

Don't be discouraged if the first contact does not develop into a full friendship. The ice has been broken, and that is an important beginning. Don't allow an initial disappointment to deter you from further attempts.

If a friendship does develop. cultivate openness and loyalty from the very first. Broken confidences mean a ruptured friendship. In your own neighbourhood, show yourself friendly, so that you will come to be accepted as part of the community.

It takes two to build a relationship and it does not always blossom overnight. Bear in mind that it is the *quality*, not the *number*, of relationships that is important. Friendship is not automatically maintained; it must be worked at.

There are various activities that can introduce one to rewarding social involvement. Volunteer groups engage in valuable social and philanthropic services—Meals on Wheels, Lifeline and similar organisations. Additional volunteers are always welcome. Volunteers to help with slow-learning children will meet a warm welcome.

In many larger cities the increase in crime has given birth to neighbourhood watch groups.

Membership in one of these would lead to friendly touch with neighbours in a non-threatening relationship.

Ideally, the church should be the place where loving care and fellowship are extended. Very often this is the case, but unfortunately that ideal is not always realised. But a growing number of churches are fully alive to the social implications of the gospel and endeavour to provide services for the suffering and unprivileged. The state, too, is paying more attention to the social needs of its citizens.

Many enduring friendships have been initiated through taking someone out for a meal. Lonely international students respond with almost pathetic eagerness to such an approach. Many never get an invitation into the home of the host country. Over a meal, conversation is relaxed and the suggested gambit of asking the guest about himself or herself, and their homeland, will meet with a warm response.

It is when we shift the focus from our own loneliness to relieving that of another sufferer, that the healing process gathers momentum in our own lives.

19

THE SPIRITUAL ELEMENT

'Where is God when I am lonely?' is a question asked by many a depressed person. It may not be actually articulated but it is there deep down nonetheless. Of course the answer is—*right beside you.*

'Whether we feel it or not,' writes M. Clarkson, 'we have His presence for our loneliness, His understanding for the human misunderstanding that ruthlessly assaults our quivering sensitivities, His unchanging and unchangeable purpose for the seeming hopelessness of our frustration and apparent uselessness . . . Our very infirmities can open up our lives to more of the power of Christ.'[1]

Scripture abounds in promises, divine undertakings that await our appropriation. There is no conceivable situation for which there is no appropriate promise. Be alert as you read the Bible, to discover what God has promised to do and then lay hold of it. Say to the Lord, 'Do as you have said.' Promises must be claimed by faith. It was by faith the patriarchs received the promises. Abraham had an abounding confidence in his God. He was 'fully assured that what He had promised He was able also to perform' (Rm 4.21).

> *'The Lord has promised good to me,*
> *His word my hope secures,*
> *He will my shield and portion be*
> *As long as life endures.*

John Newton

Some have difficulty in appropriating for them-selves the promises of the Old Testament, which were made, in the main, to Israel. They feel that to lay claim to them would be like opening a letter addressed to someone else. But Paul answers that problem:

> 'If you belong to Christ, then *you are Abraham's seed and* heirs according to the promise' (Gal 3.39: *italics mine*).

The validity of a promise depends upon the character and resources of the one who makes it. God's holy character and boundless resources make His promises credible.

'Every promise is a writing of God,' said Charles H. Spurgeon, 'which may be pleaded before Him with the reasonable request, "Do as Thou hast said." The Creator will not cheat the creature who depends upon His truth, and far more, the heavenly Father will not break His word to His own child.'[(2)]

God's promises are bound up with His character and rest on four of His attributes.

His *truth*, which renders lying impossible.

His *omniscience*, which makes His being deceived

165

or mistaken impossible.

His *immutability*, which renders change or vacillation an impossibility.

His *omnipotence*, which makes anything possible.

So, when we come to God armed with one of His promises, we can do so with the utmost confidence, for 'He who promised is faithful.' If there seems to be a yawning gap between God's promises and our experience of their fulfilment, it is because we have not bestirred ourselves to claim them.[3]

In many cases there is a condition attached to the promise. Our part is to fulfil the condition, claim the promise and expectantly await its fulfilment. It is here that we have to do battle, to 'fight the good fight of faith' against our adversary the devil who will do all in his power to dislodge us from the plane of faith. 'Satan comes and takes away the word' (Mk 4.15).

John Bunyan quaintly described his experience in endeavouring to appropriate one of the promises: 'Satan would labour to pull the promise away from me, telling me that Christ did not mean *me* in John 6.37. He pulled and I pulled. But, God be praised, I got the better of him.' Bunyan has not been alone in this representative experience.

THREE POSSIBLE ATTITUDES
We can adopt one of three attitudes in relation to God's promises:
1. We can *'come short'* of them by devaluing them to the level of our past experience (Rom 3.25 KJV). It is possible for us so to tone them down that we come far short of what God is offering.

2. We can *'stagger'* or *'waver'* because of our un-belief, either because of the risk involved or because the promise seems too good to be true (Rom 4.20). But the one who wavers misses the blessing—'That man should not think he will receive anything from the Lord' (Jas 1.7).

3. We can be *'fully assured'* of God's trustworthi-ness and receive the promises. Abraham, the father of the faithful, was 'fully assured that God had power to do what he had promised' (Rom 4.21), and therefore he 'did not waver through unbelief.'

With God, promise and performance are in-separable. So take some of the great promises of Scripture and, with them under your feet, step out in confidence. Here are some of God's undertakings which have special relevance to the problem of loneliness.

'Do not fear, *for I am with you;* do not be dismayed, for I am your God. I will strengthen you and help you; I will uphold you with my righteous hand' (Isa 41.10: *italics mine*).

'My presence will go with you, and I will give you rest' (Ex 33.14: *italics mine*).

'When you pass through the waters, *I will be with you;* and when you pass through the rivers they will not sweep over you. When you walk through the fire you will not be burned; the flames will not set you ablaze. For I am the

Lord your God . . . Do not be afraid,
for *I am with you.'* (Isa 42.2,3,5:
italics mine).

Adopt Paul's attitude toward these divine undertakings. 'I have faith in God that it will happen just
as He told me' (Ac 27.25).

20

POSITIVE STEPS TO RELIEF

Once the initial mental decision to take the initiative in establishing new relationships has been taken, positive practical steps must follow to support and implement that decision. It is so easy to yield to inertia where motivation is weak. And it is you who must supply the motivation. Already a number of possible steps have been suggested, but others follow.

The person who has a *hobby* to fall back upon is fortunate indeed. Some counsellors go so far as to assert that no man is really happy or safe without a hobby, and that it makes little difference what outside interest it is he takes up.

That statement is probably too sweeping, but there is much truth in it. Those who have cultivated no interest outside their normal work, are among the most unhappy people when they retire. Without the interest of their accustomed vocation they become bored, lonely and very sorry for themselves. But it is never too late to take up some congenial hobby.

I personally have found *gardening* the most

absorbing, refreshing and even exciting of hobbies. Few occupations can fill the lonely hours so rewardingly. To create beauty that gives both pleasure and profit to oneself and others is one of the most enjoyable and fruitful avocations.

One of the benefits of gardening as a hobby is that it has some form that is adapted to people of every age and in every stage of health. It can be engaged in outside or inside, and at any time. Even invalids can derive great enjoyment from indoor gardening.

For those blessed with good health, there are many *outdoor games* available to both men and women, at any stage of life. Apart from the enjoyment of the game itself, participation brings one into close and friendly contact with others, in a relaxed atmosphere.

Another most helpful therapy, and one that can be engaged in alone, is *walking*. 'It stimulates the respiratory system, purifies the blood, makes one feel more alive and better able to cope with life's demands.' Further, it gets one out of the house and into God's wonderful world of nature. In countries where winters are severe, many older people have even found walking under cover in a large shopping mall a health-giving and mind-refreshing exercise.

For those who are *musically inclined,* there is an abundance of music to suit every taste, either on one's own stereo or on the radio. In North America especially there are stations that specialise in Christian music on several levels. Good music is uplifting and meets our aesthetic needs.

For some who are suitably qualified, joining a *choir, orchestra* or *singing group* would, in itself, be a fulfilling experience. In addition, it is an excellent means of establishing contact with people of similar tastes.

Some with *scholastic bent* have found release and fulfilment in enrolling for a degree or other course of study which it had not been possible to take earlier in life. Many married women are adopting this avenue when their children leave home.

In the wide field of *art,* many options are open to those willing to make the venture. The author's wife discovered late in life that she had an unusual gift in painting that had lain unused for most of her life. Many of us have undiscovered talents waiting for release. In addition to painting, other options are pottery, china painting, weaving, woodwork, all forms of fancy work and many others.

Where one has the requisite skill and teaching ability, a class in some practical subject could be commenced for younger people who are unemployed, or who might otherwise be roaming the streets. A friend has turned his large garage into a woodwork shop, where he instructs young men in wood-turning and kindred work. In the process he is able to influence them for Christ.

In cities where there is an ethnic mix, there are many opportunities for helpful *ministry to immigrants or overseas students.* Two friends of the author used their home and their spare time to teach them English. As a result of their friendship and interest, a Korean and a Chinese church each had its birth in this home and are now functioning independently.

It is possible to have fellowship with the great minds of all ages and in every sphere through *read-*

ing good literature. The range of literature available in our libraries is almost unlimited. Books serious and humorous, light and heavy, educative and diverting, religious and secular are available at trifling cost.

Even if one has not had much time or taste for reading in the past, there will never be a more appropriate time to cultivate the habit than now. When physical powers wane, one can still read. Begin with books that grip and hold the interest. Then, when the reading habit has been formed, graduate to heavier and more serious subjects. It has been found that housewives who make a practice of reading are less lonely than their peers who are pursuing careers.

Where living conditions are favourable, many lonely people have found great comfort in keeping a pet, having something to love and receiving some measure of affection in return. The obvious welcome of a pet on one's return to an empty house or apartment, helps to banish loneliness.

THINK POSITIVELY

We choose what our mind feeds upon, and what we read unconsciously moulds our patterns of thought. If we surfeit our minds with negative thoughts, the result is predictable. We can programme our mental computer with thoughts that *induce* loneliness, or with thoughts that will *banish* it. This lies within our choice.

When visiting Hong Kong, a preacher was intrigued by a shop in which tattooing was done. In the window he noticed a number of mottoes which were suggested for choice. Among them was 'Born to fail.'

'But surely no one would choose that motto, would they?' he asked the Chinese tattooist.

'Yes they do,' was the reply.

'But why would they choose that one?'

The percipient reply was: 'Before they tattoo on chest, they tattoo on mind.'

Unconsciously he was giving his version of the Bible statement, 'As a man thinketh in his heart, so is he' (Prov 23.7).

Paul gives a prescription for the kind of thoughts which we should feed into our minds:

> 'Whatever is true, whatever is noble,
> whatever is right, whatever is pure,
> whatever is lovely, whatever is
> admirable—if anything is excellent or
> praiseworthy, *think about such things*'
> (Phil 4.8: *italics mine*).

Since we are commanded to think of these things, it follows that it is in our power to control our thoughts and concentrate them on positive and pleasurable concepts. They automatically exclude the opposite.

We choose the thoughts on which we will meditate, for it is our wills that control mental processes. 'A will firmly engaged with God can swing the intellectual processes around to think on holy things.'

The best thoughts to entertain are the thoughts of God. Thus, regular reading and meditating on Scriptural truth is one of the best ways to exclude thoughts that create or feed loneliness.

NOTES

Chapter 1

1. Irene M. Burnside, *Loneliness in Old Age*
   (Mental Hygiene, Volume 5, No. 3, July 1971,
   p.391)

2. David Jeremiah, *Overcoming Loneliness* (San
   Bernardino, Here's Life Publishers, 1983, p.11)

3. Tim Timmons, *Loneliness is not a Disease*
   (Eugene, Harvest House, 1981)

4. Mary Endersbee, 'All the Lonely People'
   (London, *Crusade* magazine, May 1976)

Chapter 2

1. Morris West, *The Devil's Advocate* (New York,
   Dell, 1969, p.334)

2. A.W. Tozer, *Of God and Men* (Harrisburg,
   Christian Publications 1960, pp.105, 106)

3. W.S. Hooton, *The Purpose of God for the
   Nations* (London, *Life of Faith,* 28 August 1940,
   p.489)

NOTES

4. Bernard Bangley, *The Imitation of Christ* (Crowborough, Highland, 1984, p.43)

Chapter 3

1. Ida Nell Holloway, *The Untapped Resource* (Nashville, Broadman, 1982, p.25)

2. Nicky Cruz, *Lonely, but never Alone* (Grand Rapids, Zondervan, 1981, p.59)

Chapter 4

1. Tim Timmons, *Loneliness is not a Disease* (Eugene, Harvest House, 1981, p.17)

Chapter 5

1. A.B.C. Newscast, 7.30 pm, 14 December 1983
2. William Glasser, *The Identity Society* (New York, Harper and Row, 1976, p.65)

3. Hazel Gillanders, *Treasure in an Earthen Vessel* (Melbourne, *New Life,* 23 August 1984, p.9)

Chapter 7

1. Vance Havner, *Sarah is Gone* (Chicago, *Moody Monthly,* March 1985, p.26)

2. Sheldon Vanauken, *A Severe Mercy* (London, Hodder and Stoughton, 1977, p.195)

FACING LONELINESS

Chapter 8

1. Helen Raley, *On Being a Widow* (Waco, Word Books, 1980, p.30)

2. Katie F. Wiebe, *Alone* (Wheaton, Tyndale, 1976, p.14)

3. C.S. Lewis, *A Grief Observed* (New York, Bantam, 1976, p.20)

4. Helen Raley, *Ibid*

5. Edward M. Blaiklock, *Kathleen* (London, Hodder and Stoughton, 1980, p.40)

Chapter 9

1. Timothy Stafford, *Love, Sex and the Whole Problem* (Auckland, *The Grapevine,* December 1987, p.7)

2. Craig W. Ellison, *Saying Goodbye to Loneliness* (New York, Harper and Row, 1983, p.129)

Chapter 11

1. Bruce Stabbert, *The Team Concept* (Tacoma, Hogg Brothers 1982, pp.50, 51)

Chapter 12

1. Arthur T. Pierson, *Godly Self-control* (Three Hills, Prairie, n.d. p.21)

2. O. Hallesby, *Temperament in the Christian Life* (Minneapolis, Augsburg, 1978, p.52)

3. Edgar N. Jackson, *Understanding Loneliness* (London, S.C.M. 1980, p.21)

NOTES

Chapter 13

1. William Temple, *Readings from St. John's Gospel* (London, Macmillan, 1963, p.133)

2. William E. Sangster, *The Radiant Life* (London, Hodder and Stoughton, 1957, p.91)

3. J. Gregory Mantle, *The Way of the Cross* (New York, Doran, 1922, p.20)

4. Mary Endersbee, Quoted in 'All the Lonely People' (London, *Crusade* magazine, May 1976)

5. Charles Durham, *When You're Feeling Lonely* (London, I.V.P., 1984, p.152)

Chapter 14

1. Kathleen Parsa, *Three Words* (Colorado Springs, *Discipleship,* Issue 27, 1985, p.4)

Chapter 16

1. Frederick W. Boreham, *The Luggage of Life* (London, Epworth, 1949, p.113)

2. Nancy Potts, *Living Between the Times* (Wheaton, Victor Books, 1978, p.80)

Chapter 17

1. Jerry White, *Friends and Friendship* (Colorado Springs, Nav Press, 1983, p.13)

2. 'The House by the Side of the Road' (in *Home Book of Quotations,* Dodd Mead, 1967)

3. D.W. Smith, *The Friendly Male* (Regal Books, 1983, p.5)

Chapter 18

1. Malcolm Muggeridge, *A Twentieth Century Testimony* (Nashville, Thomas Nelson, 1978, p.72)

Chapter 19

1. Margaret Clarkson, (in *Decision* magazine, March 1987)

2. Edward M. Bounds, *The Possibilities of Prayer* (New York, Revell, 1923, p.24)

3. J. Oswald Sanders, *Prayer Power Unlimited* (Chicago, Moody Press, 1947, p.45)

INDEX OF SCRIPTURES

INDEX OF NAMES